Call Them
by Their
True Names

Call Them by Their True Names

AMERICAN CRISES (AND ESSAYS)

Rebecca Solnit

Haymarket Books
Chicago, Illinois

Published in 2018 by
Haymarket Books
P.O. Box 180165
Chicago, IL 60618
773-583-7884
www.haymarketbooks.org
info@haymarketbooks.org

ISBN: 978-1-60846-946-8

Trade distribution:
In the US, Consortium Book Sales and Distribution, www.cbsd.com
In Canada, Publishers Group Canada, www.pgcbooks.ca
In the UK, Turnaround Publisher Services, www.turnaround-uk.com
All other countries, Ingram Publisher Services International,
IPS_Intlsales@ingramcontent.com

This book was published with the generous support
of Lannan Foundation and Wallace Action Fund.

Cover design by Abby Weintraub.

Printed in Canada by union labor.

Library of Congress Cataloging-in-Publication data is available.

10 9 8 7 6 5 4 3 2

Contents

IV. POSSIBILITIES

Politics and the American Language

One of the folktale archetypes, according to the Aarne-Thompson classification of these stories, tells of how "a mysterious or threatening helper is defeated when the hero or heroine discovers his name." In the deep past, people knew names had power. Some still do. Calling things by their true names cuts through the lies that excuse, buffer, muddle, disguise, avoid, or encourage inaction, indifference, obliviousness. It's not all there is to changing the world, but it's a key step.

When the subject is grim, I think of the act of naming as diagnosis. Though not all diagnosed diseases are curable, once you know what you're facing, you're far better equipped to know what you can do about it. Research, support, and effective treatment, as well as possibly redefining the disease and what it means, can proceed from this first step. Once you name a disorder, you may be able to connect to the community afflicted with it, or build one. And sometimes what's diagnosed can be cured.

Naming is the first step in the process of liberation. Calling Rumpelstiltskin by his true name makes him fly into a self-destructive rage that frees the heroine of his extortions; and though

1

fairytales are thought to be about enchantment, it's disenchant-
ment that is often the goal: breaking the spell, the illusion, the
transformation that made someone other than herself or himself,
speechless or unrecognizable or without human form. Naming
what politicians and other powerful leaders have done in secret
often leads to resignations and shifts in power.

To name something truly is to lay bare what may be brutal or
corrupt—or important or possible—and key to the work of changing the world is changing the story, the names, and inventing or
popularizing new names and terms and phrases. The project of liberation has also involved coining new terms or bringing terms that
were obscure into more popular use: we now talk about normaliza-
tion, extractivism, unburnable carbon; about walking while Black,
gaslighting, the prison-industrial complex and the new Jim Crow,
affirmative consent, cisgender, concern trolling, whataboutism, the
manosphere, and so much more.

The process works both ways. Think of the Trump administration's turning family reunification, which sounds like a good thing,
into the ominous, contagious-sounding "chain migration." Think of
the second Bush administration's redefining torture as "enhanced
interrogation," and how many press outlets went along with it.
Of the Clinton administration's hollow phrase "building a bridge
to the twenty-first century," which was supposed to celebrate the
brave new world tech would bring and disguised how much it would
return us to nineteenth-century economic divides and robber barons. Of Ronald Reagan's introduction of the figure of the "welfare
queen," a mythic being whose undeserving greed justified cutting
off aid to the poor and ignored the reality of widespread poverty.

There are so many ways to tell a lie. You can lie by ignoring
whole regions of impact, omitting crucial information, or unhitch-
ing cause and effect; by falsifying information by distortion and

disproportion, or by using names that are euphemisms for violence or slander for legitimate activities, so that the white kids are "hanging out" but the Black kids are "loitering" or "lurking." Language can erase, distort, point in the wrong direction, throw out decoys and distractions. It can bury the bodies or uncover them.

You can pretend there are two sides to the data on the climate crisis and treat corporate spin doctors as deserving of equal standing with the overwhelming majority of scientists in the field. You can just avoid connecting the dots, as this country long has done with gender violence, so that the obscene levels of domestic violence and sexual assault against women become a host of minor and unreported stories that have nothing to do with one another. You can blame the victim or reframe the story so that women are chronically dishonest or delusional rather than that they are chronically assaulted, because the former reaffirms the status quo as the latter disassembles it—which is a reminder that sometimes tearing down is constructive. There are a host of words used to damn women—*bossy, shrill, slutty, hysterical* are a few—that are rarely used for men, and other words, such as *uppity* and *exotic*, carry racial freight.

You can invent conflicts where there are none—"class versus identity politics" ignores that all of us have both, and that a majority of people who might be termed the working class are women and people of color. Occupy Wall Street's slogan "We are the 99 percent" insisted on a vision of a society that didn't need to be stratified into several classes, but in which the 1 percent—a phrase that has stuck around and become part of the mainstream vocabulary—had pitted themselves against the rest of us.

Precision, accuracy, and clarity matter, as gestures of respect toward those to whom you speak; toward the subject, whether it's an individual or the earth itself; and toward the historical record. It's also a kind of self-respect; there are many old cultures in which you are, as the saying goes, as good as your word. *Our Word Is Our Weapon* was the title of a compilation of the Zapatista Subcomandante Marcos's writings. If your word is unreliable, junk, lies, disposable pitches, you're nothing—a boy who cried wolf, a windbag, a cheat.

Or so it used to be, which is why one of the crises of this moment is linguistic. Words deteriorate into a slush of vague intention. Silicon Valley seizes on phrases to whitewash itself and push its agendas: *sharing economy, disruption, connectivity, openness*; terms like *surveillance capitalism* push back. The current president's verbal abuse of language itself, with his slurred, sloshing, semi-coherent word salad and his insistence that truth and fact are whatever he wants them to be, even if he wants them to be different from what they were yesterday: no matter what else he's serving, he's always serving meaninglessness.

The search for meaning is in how you live your life but also in how you describe it and what else is around you. As I say in one of the essays in this book, "Once we call it by name, we can start having a real conversation about our priorities and values. Because the revolt against brutality begins with a revolt against the language that hides that brutality."

Encouragement means, literally, to instill courage; *disintegration* means to lose integrity or integration. Being careful and precise about language is one way to oppose the disintegration of meaning, to encourage the beloved community and the conversations that inculcate hope and vision. Calling things by their true names is the work I have tried to do in the essays here.

I hope readers will keep in mind that these essays were written in such turbulent times that what seemed like reasonable expectations at the time of initial publication may no longer seem so.

Armpit Wax

(2014)

You can take the woman out of the church but not the church out of the woman. Or so I used to think, as my lapsed Catholic mother carried out dramas of temptation, sin, and redemption by means of ice cream and broccoli, or froze with fear at the idea of having made a mistake. She had left behind the rites and the celebrations but not the anxiety that all mistakes were unforgivable. So many of us believe in perfection, which ruins everything else, because the perfect is not only the enemy of the good, it's also the enemy of the realistic, the possible, and the fun.

My mother's punitive God was the enemy of Coyote. Prankish, lecherous, accident-prone Coyote and his cousins, the unpredictable creators of the world in Native American stories, brought me a vision of this realm as never perfect, made through collaboration and squabbling. I came across one of these stories a quarter century ago, when the conceptual artist Lewis DeSoto, whose father was Cahuilla, asked me to write about his work. He handed me a photocopy of one version of the Cahuilla creation story, which someone had transcribed from the oral tradition. The Cahuilla were one of the myriad smallish tribes that inhabited the vast area now known as California.

They lived in the western Mojave Desert, and, in the story Lewis sent me, the world begins with darkness and "beautiful, far-away sounds—sounds such as might come from distant singers." It continues, "And the earth was without form, and void; and darkness was upon the face of the deep"—not so unlike the Book of Genesis, until the maternal darkness endeavors to give birth and miscarries twice, then bears twin brothers, who grow up to quarrel constantly about who was born first.

As they fashion the world and all the things in it, the twins argue about whether there should be sickness and death. The brother who wins is worried about overpopulation. The loser abandons the earth in a huff, in his hurry leaving behind some of his creations, including coyotes, palm trees, and flies. The remaining brother becomes such a problem—lusting after his daughter, the moon; giving rattlesnakes poisonous fangs; arming people with weapons they would use against each other—that his creatures have to figure out how to kill him. No one is unequivocally good, starting with the gods.

Where I live, in the San Francisco Bay Area, the Ohlone people say that Coyote was the first being, and the world was created by him, and by Eagle and by Hummingbird, who laughs at Coyote's attempts to figure out just where to impregnate his wife. (He's not always this naïve. In the Winnebago stories from the Great Lakes, Coyote sends his detachable penis on long, sneaky missions in pursuit of penetration, like some drone from the dreamtime.) As the Californian poet Gary Snyder once put it, "Old Doctor Coyote...is not inclined to make a distinction between good and evil." Instead, he's full of contagious exuberance and great creative force. In another Californian creation myth, the gods argue about procreation: one thinks a man and woman should put a stick between them at night, and it will be a baby when they wake up. The other says that there should be a lot of nocturnal embracing and laughing in the baby-making process.

These supple stories, unalarmed by improvisation, failure, and sex, remind me of jazz. In contrast, the creator in the Old Testament is a tyrannical composer whose score can only be performed one right way. The angel with the flaming sword drove us out of Eden because we talked to snakes and made a bad choice about fruit snacks. Everything that followed was an affliction and a curse. Redemption was required, because perfection was the standard by which everything would be measured. And by which everything falls short.

Nearly everyone under the influence of Genesis, over half of the world's population, believes in some version of the fall from grace. Even secular stories tend to be structured that way. Conservatives have their Eden before the fall—it usually involves strong fathers and demure women and nonexistent queer people—and liberals also have stories about when everything was uncorrupted, about matriarchal communities and Paleo diets and artisanal just about anything, from cheese to chairs. But if you give up on grace, you can give up on the fall. You can start enjoying stuff that's only pretty good.

According to the Pomo, another Northern California tribe, the world was formed when the creator rolled his armpit wax into a ball. Or, according to the Maidu, who live largely in the northern Sierra Nevada Mountains, it's made from mud picked out from under the nails of a turtle who'd scraped it up at the bottom of the primordial soup.

They're not my property, these old stories, but they're an invitation to reconsider the stories that are. If the perfect is the enemy of the good, maybe imperfection is its friend.

I.
Electoral Catastrophes

The Loneliness
of Donald Trump

(2017)

Once upon a time, a child was born into wealth and wanted for nothing, but he was possessed by bottomless, endless, grating, grasping
wanting, and wanted more, and got it, and more after that, and
always more. He was a pair of ragged orange claws upon the ocean
floor, forever scuttling, pinching, reaching for more, a carrion crab,
a lobster and a boiling lobster pot in one, a termite, a tyrant over his
own little empires. He got a boost at the beginning from the wealth
handed him and then moved among grifters and mobsters who cut
him slack as long as he was useful; or maybe there's slack in arenas
where people live by personal loyalty until they betray or are betrayed, and don't live by the law or the book. So, for seven decades,
he fed his appetites and exercised his license to lie, cheat, steal, and
stiff working people of their wages, made messes, left them behind,
grabbed more baubles, and left things in ruin.

 He was supposed to be a great maker of things, but he was
mostly a breaker. He acquired buildings and women and enterprises and treated them all alike, promoting and deserting them, run-

ning into bankruptcies and divorces, treading on lawsuits the way lumberjacks of old walked across the logs floating down the river to the mill, but as long as he moved in his underworld of dealmakers, the rules were wobbly and the enforcement wobblier, and he could stay afloat. But his appetite was endless, and he wanted more, so he gambled to become the most powerful man in the world, and won, careless of what he wished for.

Thinking of him, I think of Pushkin's retelling of the fairytale "The Fisherman and the Golden Fish." After being caught in the old fisherman's net, the golden fish speaks up and offers wishes in return for being thrown back in the sea. The fisherman asks him for nothing, though later he tells his wife of his chance encounter with the magical creature. The fisherman's wife sends him back to ask for a new washtub for her, and then a second time to ask for a cottage to replace their hovel, and the wishes are granted. As she grows prouder and greedier, she sends him to ask that she become a wealthy person in a mansion with servants, whom she abuses, and then she sends her husband back. The old man grovels before the fish, caught between the shame of the requests and the appetite of his wife, and she becomes tsarina and has her boyards and nobles drive the husband from her palace. You could call the husband consciousness—the awareness of others and of oneself in relation to others—and the wife craving.

Finally, she wishes to be supreme over the seas and over the fish itself, endlessly uttering wishes, and the old man goes back to the sea to tell the fish—to complain to the fish—of this latest round of wishes. The fish this time doesn't even speak, just flashes its tail, and the old man turns around to see, on the shore, his wife with her broken washtub at their old hovel. Overreach is perilous, says this Russian tale; enough is enough. And too much is nothing.

The child who became the most powerful man in the world, or at least occupied the real estate occupied by a series of those men, had run a family business and then starred in an unreality show based on the fiction that he was a stately emperor of enterprise, rather than a buffoon, and each was a hall of mirrors made to flatter his sense of self, the one edifice he kept raising higher and higher and never abandoned.

I have often run across men (and rarely, but not never, women) who have become so powerful that there is no one around to tell them when they are cruel, wrong, foolish, absurd, repugnant. In the end there is no one else in their world, because when you are not willing to hear how others feel, what others need, when you do not care, you are not willing to acknowledge others' existence. That's how it's lonely at the top. It is as if these petty tyrants live in a world without honest mirrors, without others, without gravity, and they are buffered from the consequences of their failures.

"They were careless people," F. Scott Fitzgerald wrote of the rich couple at the heart of *The Great Gatsby*. "They smashed up things and creatures and then retreated back into their money or their vast carelessness, or whatever it was that kept them together, and let other people clean up the mess they had made." Some of us are surrounded by destructive people who tell us we're worthless when we're endlessly valuable, that we're stupid when we're smart, that we're failing even when we succeed. But the opposite of people who drag you down isn't people who build you up and butter you up. It's equals who are generous but keep you accountable, true mirrors who reflect back who you are and what you are doing.

We keep each other honest, we keep each other good with our feedback, our intolerance of meanness and falsehood, our demands that the people we are with listen, respect, respond—as we are allowed to, if we are free and valued ourselves. There is a democracy of social discourse, in which we are reminded that, just as we are beset with desires and fears and feelings, so are others. There was an old woman in Occupy Wall Street whose words I always go back to, who said, "We're fighting for a society in which everyone is important." That's what a democracy of mind and heart, as well as of economy and polity, would look like.

In the aftermath of Trump's triumph, Hannah Arendt has become alarmingly relevant, and her books have been selling well, particularly *On the Origins of Totalitarianism*. Scholar Lyndsey Stonebridge pointed out to Krista Tippett, on the radio show *On Being*, that Arendt advocated for the importance of an inner dialogue with oneself, for a critical splitting in which you interrogate yourself—for a real conversation between the fisherman and his wife, you could say. She concluded, "People who can do that can actually then move on to having conversations with other people and then judging with other people. And what [Arendt] called 'the banality of evil' was the inability to hear another voice, the inability to have a dialogue either with oneself or the imagination to have a dialogue with the world, the moral world."

Some use their power to silence that dialogue and live in the void of their own increasingly deteriorating, off-course sense of self and meaning. It's like going mad on a desert island, only with sycophants and room service. It's like having a compliant compass that agrees north is wherever you want it to be. The tyrant of a family, the tyrant of a little business or a huge enterprise, the tyrant of a nation—power corrupts, and absolute power often corrupts the awareness of those who possess it. Or reduces it: narcissists, sociopaths, and egomaniacs are people for whom others don't exist.

We gain awareness of ourselves and others from setbacks and difficulties; we get used to a world that is not always about us; and those who do not have to cope with that are brittle, weak, unable to endure contradiction, convinced of the necessity of always having one's own way. The rich kids I met in college were flailing as though they wanted to find walls around them, leaping from their inherited heights as though they wanted there to be gravity and to hit the ground, but parents and privilege kept throwing out safety nets and buffers, kept padding the walls and picking up the pieces, so that all their acts were meaningless, literally inconsequential. They floated like astronauts in outer space.

Equality keeps us honest. Our peers remind us who we are and how we are doing, providing that service in personal life that a free press does in a functioning society. Inequality creates liars and delusion. The powerless are forced to dissemble—that's how slaves, servants, and women got the reputation of being liars—and the powerful grow stupid on the lies they require from their subordinates and on their lack of need to know about others who are nobody, who don't count, who've been silenced or trained to please. This is why I pair privilege with obliviousness; obliviousness is privilege's form of deprivation. When you don't hear others, they become unreal, and you are left in the wasteland of a world with only yourself in it. That surely makes you starving, though you know not for what, if you have ceased to imagine that others exist in any true, deep way. This need for egalitarian contact is one for which we hardly have language, or at least lack a familiar conversation.

A man wished to become the most powerful man in the world, and by happenstance and intervention and a series of disasters was granted his wish. Surely he must have imagined that more power meant more flattery, a grander image, a greater hall of mirrors reflecting back his magnificence. But he misunderstood power and prominence. This man had bullied friends and acquaintances, wives and servants, and he bullied facts and truths, insistent that he was more than they were, than truth is, that truth, too, must yield to his will. It did not, but the people he bullied pretended that it did. Or perhaps it was that he was a salesman, throwing out one pitch after another, abandoning each one as soon as it left his mouth. A hungry ghost always wants the next thing, not the last thing.

This man imagined that the power would repose within him and make him great, a Midas touch that would turn all to gold. But the power of the presidency was what it had always been: a system of relationships, a power that rested on people's willingness to carry out the orders the president gave, a willingness that came from the president's respect for the rule of law, truth, and the people. A man who gives an order that is not followed has his powerlessness hung out like dirty laundry. One day early in his tenure, one of this president's minions announced that the president's power would not be questioned. There are tyrants who might utter such a statement and strike fear into those beneath him, because they have instilled enough fear.

A true tyrant does not depend on cooperative power but issues commands, enforced by thugs, goons, Stasi, the SS, or death squads. A true tyrant has subordinated the system of government and made it loyal to himself rather than to the system of laws or the ideals of the country. This would-be tyrant didn't understand that he was in a system where many who worked in government—perhaps most, beyond the members of his party in the legislative branch—were loyal to law and principle, and not to him. White House aide Stephen Miller announced that the president would not be questioned, and we laughed. The president called in, like courtiers, the heads of the FBI, of the NSA, and the director of national intelligence, his own legal counsel, to tell them to suppress evidence, to stop investigations, and found that their loyalty was not to him. He found out to his chagrin that we were still something of a republic, and that the free press could not be so easily stopped; the public itself refuses to be cowed and mocks him earnestly at every turn.

A true tyrant sits beyond the sea, in Pushkin's country. He corrupts elections in his country, eliminates his enemies (journalists, in particular) with bullets, poisons, with mysterious deaths made to look like accidents—he spreads fear and bullies the truth successfully, strategically. Though he too overreached, with his intrusions into the American election, and what he had hoped would be invisible caused the whole world to scrutinize him and his actions, history, and impact with concern and even fury. Russia may have ruined whatever standing and trust it had, may have exposed itself, with its interventions in the US and European elections.

The American buffoon's commands were disobeyed, his secrets leaked at such a rate his office resembled the fountains at Versailles, or maybe just a sieve. Not long into his time in office, an extraordinary piece was published in the *Washington Post* with *thirty* anonymous sources. His agenda was undermined, even by a minority party that was not supposed to have much in the way of power; the judiciary kept suspending his executive orders; and scandals erupted like boils and sores. Inhabitants of the United States engaged in many kinds of resistance, inside and outside the arenas of electoral politics, at unprecedented levels. The dictator of the little demimondes of beauty pageants, casinos, luxury condominiums, fake universities offering fake educations with real debt, fake reality TV in which he was master of the fake fate of others, an arbiter of all worth and meaning, became fortune's fool.

He is the most mocked man in the world. After the Women's March on January 21, 2017, people joked that he had been rejected by more women in one day than any man in history; he was mocked in newspapers, on television, in cartoons, by foreign leaders; was the butt of a million jokes; and his every tweet was instantly met with an onslaught of attacks and insults from ordinary citizens, gleeful to be able to speak sharp truth to bloated power.

He is the old fisherman's wife who wished for everything, and sooner or later he will end up with nothing. The wife sitting in front of her hovel was poorer after her series of wishes because she now owned not only her poverty but also her mistakes and her destructive pride, because she might have done otherwise but brought power and glory crashing down upon her, because she had made her bed badly and was lying in it.

The man in the White House sits, naked and obscene, a pustule of ego, in the harsh light, a man whose grasp exceeded his understanding because his understanding was dulled by indulgence. He must know somewhere below the surface he skates on that he has destroyed his image, and, like Dorian Gray, will be devoured by his own corrosion in due time, too. One way or another this will kill him, though he may drag down millions with him. One way or another, he knows he has stepped off a cliff, pronounced himself king of the air, and is in free-fall. A dung heap awaits his landing; the dung is all his; when he plunges into it he will be, at last, a self-made man.

CODA (JULY 16, 2018)

I wrote this coda on July 16, 2018, the morning that Trump emerged from his private meeting with Vladimir Putin and shocked the world (even if he didn't surprise most of us) with his overt deference to the latter:

Once upon a time a man made a pact. He would be king of the world, or would appear to be, but only by letting a menacing man be king of him, a king who held all his secrets and records and could unmake him at any moment. He lorded and gloated and boasted and swam downstream in his own greasy self-regard until it was time to meet his maker, and in a private session his maker fixed him with a glittering eye and reminded him what was what and who owned him, and where the bodies were buried. They were buried in an open grave, and the grave itself grinned up at him, showing its pearly gravestone-teeth.

He came out of that room knowing that to be the king of everything but himself was to be no king at all but someone's pawn, and at that moment his leash felt very short and his collar very tight and his lordliness a mockery. He was sad and miserable and cowed, and crawled out of the chamber, and his usually whining, preening, shouting voice was defeated and flat and fearful. His king looked on him balefully, indulgently, smiling like a cat looking at its kill, and none of the monsters in the name of Jesus around him had ever thought to ask him at any crucial juncture what profiteth a man if he gains the whole world but sells his soul to someone who might come collecting in this lifetime?

His followers turned away—scurried away to denounce him—for he had not gone anywhere new, but the world now saw that he had gone too far into the trap of the Cheshire cat grinning next to him, and they no longer dared be there with him or deny that it was a trap. That was a day that ended his era and began a new one, the one of his downfall that would be as dramatic and strange and unforeseen as his rise. That was a day his followers made statements that were new traps, traps to prevent them from going back to their old lies to exculpate him, and they began to try to wash themselves of his crimes, but the stains were who they were. They were trying to wash themselves of themselves. But the servants and former servants of the government he more or less headed—the people of his administration he had insulted again and again when they told the truth of what he lost that he might win his office—rose up and condemned him, one after the other, as a traitor, a liar, a fool, a saboteur of everything he was supposed to shepherd.

Something changed that day, a shift that was as huge and tangible as it was incalculable. Or perhaps it would be calculable when the histories of the next few years were written, but on that day they could hardly be imagined.

Milestones in Misogyny

(2016)

Women told me they had flashbacks to hideous episodes in their past after the second presidential debate on October 9, 2016, or couldn't sleep, or had nightmares. The words in that debate mattered, as did their delivery. Donald Trump interrupted Hillary Clinton eighteen times (compared to fifty-one interruptions in the first debate). His reply to moderator Anderson Cooper's question about the videotaped boasts, released a few days earlier, of his grabbing women "by the pussy," was this: "But it's locker room talk, and it's one of those things. I will knock the hell out of ISIS... And we should get on to much more important things and much bigger things." Then he promised to "make America safe again"—but not from him. That week, women and ISIS were informally paired, as things Trump promised to assault.

One of the most extraordinary days in recent American history was October 7, 2016, when the Obama administration made a public announcement that the Putin regime was meddling in the US election. This should have been earthshaking news, but it was quickly eclipsed by the release of the *Access Hollywood* tape, whose salacious nastiness grabbed the media's attention instead; that was, in turn, pushed out of the center of attention by Wikileaks' release of hacked DNC emails, which a more a diligent media might have connected back to the Obama administration's warning.

But words were secondary to actions. Trump roamed, loomed, glowered, snarled, and appeared to copulate with his podium, grasping it with both hands and swaying his hips, seeming briefly lost in reverie. The menace was so dramatic, so Hitchcockian, that the Hollywood composer Danny Elfman wrote a soundtrack for a video edit that played up the most ominous moments. "Watching Trump lurching behind Hillary during the debate felt a bit like a zombie movie," Elfman said. "Like at any moment he was going to attack her, rip off her head, and eat her brains." Friends told me they thought he might assault her; I thought it possible myself as I watched him roam and rage. He was, as we sometimes say, in her space, and her ability to remain calm and on-message seemed heroic. Like many men throughout the election, he appeared to be outraged that she was in it. The election, that is. And her space.

In the ninety-minute debate, Trump lurched around the stage, gaslighting, discrediting, interrupting, often to insist that Clinton was lying or just to drown out her words and her voice; sexually shaming (this was the debate in which he tried to find room in his family box for three women who had accused Bill Clinton of sexual harassment or assault); and threatening to throw her in prison. Earlier in the campaign he'd urged his supporters to shoot her. "Hillary wants to abolish, essentially abolish the Second Amendment," he rumbled at one of his rage-inciting rallies, following a patent untruth with a casual threat: "By the way, if she gets to pick her judges, nothing you can do, folks. Although the Second Amendment people, maybe there is, I don't know." At the Republican Convention, former New Jersey governor Chris Christie led chants of "Lock her up!" In the spring, Trump retweeted a supporter who asked: "If Hillary Clinton can't satisfy her husband what makes her think she can satisfy America?" Perhaps the president is married to the nation in some mystical way; if so,

America was about to become a battered woman, badgered, lied to, threatened, gaslighted, betrayed, and robbed by a grifter.

Trump is patriarchy unbuttoned, paunchy, in a baggy suit, with his hair oozing and his lips flapping and his face squinching into clownish expressions of mockery and rage and self-congratulation. He picked as a running mate buttoned-up patriarchy, the lean, crop-haired, perpetually tense Mike Pence, who actually has experience in government, signing eight antiabortion bills in his four years as governor of Indiana, and going after Planned Parenthood the way Trump went after hapless beauty queens. The Republican platform was, as usual, keen to gut reproductive rights and pretty much any rights that appertained to people who weren't straight, or male, or white.

Misogyny was everywhere. It came from the right and the left, and Clinton was its bull's-eye, but it spilled over to women across the political spectrum. Early on, some of Trump's fury focused on the Fox presenter Megyn Kelly, who had questioned him about his derogatory comments on some women's appearances. He made the bizarre statement on CNN that "you could see there was blood coming out of her eyes. Blood coming out of her wherever." He also denigrated his opponents' wives and Republican primary opponent Carly Fiorina's face; in a flurry of middle-of-the-night tweets he obligingly attacked Alicia Machado, a former Miss Universe, after Clinton baited him about his treatment of Machado; he attacked the women who, after the "grab them by the pussy" tape was released, accused him of having assaulted them.

Trump's surrogates and key supporters constituted a sort of misogyny army—or as Star Jones, a former host of *The View*, put it, "Newt Gingrich, Giuliani, and Chris Christie: they've got like the trifecta of misogyny." The army included Steve Bannon, who, as head of the alt-right site Breitbart News, hired Milo Yiannopoulos and helped merge the misogynistic fury of the men's rights movement with white supremacy and anti-Semitism to form a new cabal of far-right fury. Roger Ailes—following his dismissal from Fox News in July 2016, after more than two dozen women testified about his decades-long sexual harassment, grotesque degradation, and exploitation of his female employees—became Trump's debate coach, though they soon fell out; some reports said Ailes was frustrated by Trump's inability to concentrate. Fox anchor Andrea Tantaros claimed that, under Ailes, Fox was "a sex-fueled, Playboy Mansion–like cult, steeped in intimidation, indecency, and misogyny." It seems telling that the rise of the far right and the fall of truthful news were, to a meaningful extent, engineered by a television network that was also a miserable one-man brothel. But that old right-wing men are misogynists is about as surprising as that alligators bite.

Clinton was constantly berated for qualities rarely mentioned in male politicians, including ambition—something, it's safe to assume, she has in common with everyone who ever ran for elected office. It was possible, according to a headline in *Psychology Today*, that she was "pathologically ambitious." She was criticized for having a voice. While Bernie Sanders railed and Trump screamed and snickered, Fox commentator Brit Hume complained about Clinton's "sharp, lecturing tone," which, he said, was "not so attractive"; MSNBC's Lawrence O'Donnell gave her public instructions on how to use a microphone; Bob Woodward bitched that she was "screaming"; and Bob Cusack, the editor of the political newspaper the *Hill*, said, "When Hillary Clinton raises her voice, she loses." One could get the impression that a woman should campaign in a sultry whisper, but, of course, if she did that she would not project power. But if she did project power she would fail as a woman, since power, in this framework, is a male prerogative, which is to say that the setup was not intended to include women.

As Sady Doyle noted, "She can't be sad or angry, but she *also* can't be happy or amused, and she also can't refrain from expressing any of those emotions. There is literally no way out of this one. Anything she does is wrong." One merely had to imagine a woman candidate doing what Trump did, from lying to leering, to understand what latitude masculinity possesses. "No advanced step taken by women has been so bitterly contested as that of speaking in public," Susan B. Anthony said in 1900. "For nothing which they have attempted, not even to secure the suffrage, have they been so abused, condemned and antagonized." Or, as Mary Beard put it a few years ago, "We have never escaped a certain male cultural desire for women's silence."

Trump harped on the theme that Clinton had been in power for thirty years, seeming to equate her person with feminism or liberalism or some other inchoate force that he intended to defeat, and in these narratives her power seemed huge and transcendent, looming over the nation the way he'd loomed over her in the second debate. By figures on both the right and the left, Clinton was held to be more responsible for her husband's policies than he was, more responsible for the war in Iraq than the rarely mentioned Bush administration, responsible for Obama's policies as though he had carried out her agenda rather than she his. These narratives cast her as a demoness with unlimited powers, or as a wicked woman, because she'd had power and aspired to have power again. One got the impression that any power a woman had was too much, and that a lot of men found women very scary.

Clinton's very existence seemed to infuriate a lot of people, as it has since at least 1992. It's complicated to talk about misogyny and Clinton, because she is a complex figure who has been many things over the decades. There are certainly reasons to disagree with and dislike things she has said and done, but that doesn't explain the overwrought emotionality that swirls around her. Raised as a conservative (and hated by some on the left during this campaign for having been a "Goldwater Girl," though she had stumped for him as a nonvoting high school student), she soon became a radical who campaigned for the most left-leaning Democratic candidates in 1968 and 1972, registered Latinx voters in Texas in the latter election; wrote a thesis on Saul Alinsky, who afterward offered her a job; advocated for rights for women and children; then shifted right in the 1980s, perhaps to adapt to the political climate of her husband's home state of Arkansas or to the Reagan era.

You could pick out a lot of feminist high points and corporate and neoliberal low points in her career, but for anyone more interested in the future of the United States and the world, her 2016 platform seemed most relevant, though no one seemed to know anything about it. The main networks devoted only thirty-two minutes to the candidates' platforms amid the hundreds of hours of election coverage. Lots of politicians have been disliked for their policies and positions, but Clinton's were often close to Sanders's, and similar to, or to the left of, every high-profile male Democrat in recent years, including her husband; Barack Obama; Joe Biden; John Kerry; and Howard Dean. But what had been accepted or merely disliked in them was an outrage in her, and whatever resentment they'd elicited was faint compared to the hysterical rage that confronted her as, miraculously, she continued to march forward.

Trump's slogan, "Make America great again," seemed to invoke a return to a Never Never Land of white male supremacy, where coal was an awesome fuel, blue-collar manufacturing jobs were what they had been in 1956, women belonged in the home, and the needs of white men were paramount. After the election, many on the left joined the chorus, assuring us that Clinton lost because she hadn't paid enough attention to the so-called white working class—a term that, given that she wasn't being berated for ignoring women, seemed to be a code word for white men. These men were more responsible than any group for Trump's victory (63 percent of them voted for him; 31 percent for Clinton).

One might argue she lost because of the disenfranchisement of millions of people of color through long-plotted Republican strategies: cutting the number of polling stations; limiting voting hours; harassing and threatening would-be voters; introducing voter ID laws such as the Crosscheck program, which made it a lot harder for people of color to register to vote. Or because of the smearing intervention by FBI director James Comey ten days before the election; or because of years of negative media coverage; or because of foreign intervention designed to sabotage her chances; or because of misogyny. But instead we heard two stories about why she lost (and almost none about why, despite everything, she won the popular vote by almost three million votes, a total exceeding the votes won by any white man, ever, in a US election).

The We Must Pay More Attention to the White Working Class analysis said that Clinton lost because she did not pay enough attention to white men. Those wielding it didn't seem interested in the 37 percent of Americans who aren't white, or the 51 percent who are women. I've always had the impression—from TV, movies, newspapers, sports, books, my education, my personal life, and my knowledge of who owns most things and holds government office at every level in my country—that white men get a lot of attention already.

The other story was about white women, who voted 43 percent for Clinton to 53 percent for Trump. We were excoriated for voting for Trump, on the grounds that all women, but only women, should be feminists. That there are a lot of women in the United States who are not feminists does not surprise me. To be a feminist you have to believe in your equality and rights, which can make your life unpleasant and dangerous if you live in a family, a community, a church, a state that does not agree with you about this. For many women it's safer not to have those beliefs in this country, where a woman is beaten every eleven seconds or so and women's partners and exes are the leading cause of injury to women from their teens through forties. And those beliefs are not universally available in a country where feminism is forever being demonized and distorted. It seems it's also worse to vote for a racist if you're a woman, because while white women were excoriated, white men were let off the hook (across every racial category, more men than women voted for Trump; overall, 54 percent of women supported Clinton; 53 percent of men voted for Trump).

So women were hated for not having gender loyalty. But here's the fun thing about being a woman: we were also hated for having gender loyalty. Women were accused of voting with their reproductive parts if they favored the main female candidate, though most men throughout American history have favored male candidates without being accused of voting with their penises. Penises were only discussed during a Republican primary debate, when Marco Rubio suggested Trump's was small and Trump boasted that it wasn't. "I don't vote with my vagina," the actress Susan Sarandon announced, then voted for the Green Party candidate, Jill Stein, who one might think was just as vagina-y a candidate as Clinton but apparently wasn't.

"One of the many lessons of the recent presidential election campaign and its repugnant outcome," Mark Lilla wrote in the *New York Times*, "is that the age of identity liberalism must be brought to an end." He condemned Clinton for calling out explicitly to Black, Latino, LGBT, and women voters at every stop. "This," he said, "was a strategic mistake. If you are going to mention groups in America, you had better mention all of them." Who's not on that list, though it's one that actually covers the majority of Americans? Heterosexual white men, notably, since it's hard to imagine Lilla was put out that Clinton neglected Asians and Native Americans.

"Identity politics" has become a dismissive term for talking about race or gender or sexual orientation, which is very much the way we've talked about liberation over the last 160 years in the United States. By that measure Frederick Douglass, Harriet Tubman, Elizabeth Cady Stanton, Susan B. Anthony, Ida B. Wells, Rosa Parks, Bella Abzug, Ella Baker, Bayard Rustin, Malcolm X, Winona LaDuke, Vine DeLoria, Del Martin, and Harvey Milk were just lowly practitioners of the identity politics we've been told to get over. Shortly after the election Bernie Sanders, who'd gotten on the no–identity politics bandwagon, explained: "It is not good enough to say, 'Hey, I'm a Latina, vote for me.' That is not good enough. I have to know whether that Latina is going to stand up with the working class of this country.... It is not good enough for someone to say: 'I'm a woman, vote for me.' No, that's not good enough." In fact, Clinton never said that, though one could argue that Trump had said, incessantly, aggressively, "I'm a white man, vote for me," and even that Sanders had implicitly conveyed that same message or benefitted from it without having to put it in words. *Vox* journalist David Roberts did a word-frequency analysis of Clinton's campaign speeches and concluded that she mostly talked about workers, jobs, education, and the economy, exactly the things she was berated for neglecting. She mentioned jobs almost six hundred times, and racism, women's rights, and abortion a few dozen times each. But she was portrayed as talking about her gender all the time, though it was everyone else who couldn't shut up about it.[1]

How the utopian idealism roused by Sanders's promises in the winter of 2015 morphed so quickly into a Manichean hatred of

---

1. A year later Danica Roem, a transgender candidate who won election to the Virginia House of Delegates, noted, "I talked relentlessly about jobs. Roads. Schools. Health care. Equality. I know this because Lee [Carter] and I saw each other on the stump constantly. And y'all went after us for [that] and 'teaching transgenderism to kindergartners' and 'socialism.'"

Clinton as the anti-Bernie was one of the mysteries of this mysteriously horrific election, but that raging, loathing hatred was so compelling that many people seemed to wake up from the Democratic primary only when Trump won the general election; they had until then believed Clinton was still running against Sanders. Or they believed that she was an inevitable presence, like Mom, so they could hate her with confidence and she would win anyway. Many around me loved Sanders with what came to seem an unquestioning religious devotion and hated Clinton even more fervently. The hatred on the right spilled over into actual violence over and over again at Trump rallies, but the left also had its share of vitriol.

I had seen all around me a mob mentality, an irrational groupthink that fed on itself, confirmed itself, and punished doubt, opposition, or complexity. I thought of the two-minute group hate sessions in *1984*:

> The horrible thing about the Two Minutes Hate was not that one was obliged to act a part, but that it was impossible to avoid joining in. Within thirty seconds any pretense was always unnecessary. A hideous ecstasy of fear and vindictiveness, a desire to kill, to torture, to smash faces in with a sledge hammer, seemed to flow through the whole group of people like an electric current, turning one even against one's will into a grimacing, screaming lunatic. And yet the rage that one felt was an abstract, undirected emotion which could be switched from one object to another like the flame of a blowlamp.

That emotion was directed at Clinton and was ready to swerve toward anyone who supported her, accompanied by accusations of treason and other kinds of invective. Many supporters fell silent or took to supporting her in secret, which is not the kind of support a candidate needs. A San Franciscan friend wrote:

> Every woman I know and almost every journalist or opinion writer who planned to vote for her included in every single pos-

itive statement about her—everything from Facebook posts to lengthy major media articles—something to the effect of "She is, of course, not a perfect candidate, but ..." or "I, of course, have serious problems with some aspects of her record, but ..." It became the boilerplate you had to include to forestall the worst of the rage-trolls (inevitably eventually someone would pop up anyway to accuse you of trying to shove your queen's coronation down everyone's throat, but at least the boilerplate delayed it).

◆

Mentioning that Clinton had won the popular vote upset many of the men I am in contact with, though they would not or could not conceive of it that way. I wrote at the time: "With their deep belief in their own special monopoly on objectivity, slightly too many white men assure me that there is no misogyny in their subjective assessments or even no subjectivity and no emotion driving them, and there are no grounds for other opinions since theirs is not an opinion." Then these men went back to talking about what a loser Clinton was, a perspective that seemed to erotically stimulate them in the same way that her possible victory seemed to elicit an erotic and deeply emotional loathing.

There was considerable evidence that we had not had a free and fair election, evidence that might have allowed us to contest it and to stop Trump. But these men of the left were so dedicated to Clinton's status as a loser that they wanted Trump to win, because it vindicated something that went deeper than their commitment to almost anything else. They insisted on a tautology—that Clinton lost because she was a loser—and dismissed all other factors. Trump was the candidate so weak that his minority victory[2]

---

2. If he won. I wrote later: "In many swing states, including Florida, North Carolina, Pennsylvania, and Wisconsin, there were extraordinary discrepancies between the exit polls and the vote tallies. Though it's common to regard the

was only possible because of the disenfranchisement of millions of voters of color; the end of the Voting Rights Act; a long-running right-wing campaign to make Clinton's use of a private email server, surely the dullest and most uneventful scandal in history, an epic crime; and the late intervention, with apparent intent to sabotage, of FBI director James Comey. We found out via Comey's outrageous gambit that it is more damaging to be a woman with an aide who has an estranged husband who is a creep than to be an actual predator charged by more than a dozen women with groping and sexual assault.

Hillary Clinton was all that stood between us and a reckless, unstable, ignorant, inane, infinitely vulgar, climate change–denying, white nationalist misogynist with authoritarian ambitions and kleptocratic plans. A lot of people, particularly white men, could not bear her, and that is as good a reason as any for Trump's victory. Over and over again, I heard men declare that she had failed to make them vote for her. They saw the loss as hers rather than ours, and they blamed her for it, as though election was a gift they withheld from her because she did not deserve it or did not attract them. They did not blame themselves or the electorate or the system for failing to stop Trump.

---

latter as more reliable than the former, in other parts of the world exit polls are treated as important verifications of the outcome. Clinton would have won the election overwhelmingly, had she won those states. Perhaps she did. Shortly after the election, Bob Fitrakis and Harvey Wasserman reported: 'In 24 of 28 states, unadjusted exit polls also showed Clinton with vote counts significantly higher than the final official outcome. The likelihood of this happening in an election that is not rigged [is] in the realm of virtual statistical impossibility.' I don't know if their statement is accurate, because there has been no significant investigation, and the recount in Michigan, Wisconsin, and Pennsylvania, initiated by Jill Stein, was stopped by a clearly panicked Republican Party."

Twenty Million Missing Storytellers

(2018)

Most new ideas begin in the margins or shadows and move toward the center. They are often something that a few people thought, something that seemed radical or edgy or a bit too much, or just something hardly anyone noticed or felt strongly about. If they were ideas about justice, they were considered extreme or unrealistic. Then the idea kept traveling, and by the end of the journey it was what everyone always thought. Or, rather, what they *thought* they had always thought, because it's convenient to ignore that they used to not pay attention or had thought something completely different, something that now looks like discrimination or cluelessness. A new idea is like a new species: it evolves; it expands its habitat; it changes the ecosystem around it; and then it fits in as though it was always there, as though we as a nation had always condemned slavery or believed women deserved the vote or thought nonstraight people were entitled to the same rights as straight people.

In the fall of 2017, we began to consider anew how violence, hate, and discrimination push people out, and how the stories we have are haunted by the ghosts of the stories we never got. This was a key part of the analysis of what the gendered violence of Harvey Weinstein and other powerful men in Hollywood had accomplished. Rebecca Traister was one of the people to say it early, when she wrote:

> The accused are men who help to determine what art gets seen and appreciated—and, crucially, paid for. They decide whose stories get brought to screens.... They are also the men with the most power to determine what messages get sent about politicians to a country that then chooses between those politicians in elections.... We cannot retroactively resituate the women who left jobs, who left their whole careers because the navigation of the risks, these daily diminutions and abuses, drove them out. Nor can we retroactively see the movies they would have made or the art they would have promoted, or read the news as they might have reported it.

Many people, including Traister and Jill Filipovic, noted that some of the most powerful men in US media had been exposed as serial sexual harassers, and that these men—including Charlie Rose, Matt Lauer, and Mark Halperin—had shaped the hostile narrative around Hillary Clinton. The idea that had begun with the men who decided who would make movies and what stories we would hear moved on to the men who decided how politicians would be depicted and what would be emphasized (Clinton's emails) and what wouldn't (Trump's mob ties, lies, bankruptcies, lawsuits, sexual assaults). It shaped an election; you can imagine another outcome, had other people been in charge of framing it.

By the end of 2017, Richard Brody in the *New Yorker* found this way of framing our current situation so compelling he foregrounded it in his write-up of the year's best movies, not usually a place for suggesting radical political reform. That the idea arrived there is a sign of how far it traveled, and how fast, during the fall. Brody declared,

> Any list of the year's best movies has gaps—of the movies, performances, and other creations that are missing because they are unrealized, unrealized because the women (and, yes, also some men) who were working their way up to directing, producing, or other notable activities in the world of movies, who were already acting or writing or fulfilling other creative positions, had their careers derailed when they were threatened, intimidated, silenced, or otherwise detached from the industry by powerful men abusing their power for their own pleasure and advantage.

The absence had become present in a lot of minds.

But who is missing from the American narrative? It's not only the women directors, the Black screenwriters, the not-so-misogynist lead journalists in the mainstream.

It's voters.

Voting is a form of speech, a way to say what you believe in, what kind of world you want to see. Having a voice doesn't just mean literally being able to say things; it means having a role, having agency, being able to say things that have an impact whether it's "I witnessed this police brutality" or "No, I don't want to have sex with you" or "This is my vision of society."

As far as I can estimate, about twenty million voters were disenfranchised in the last election. Voter ID laws, the Crosscheck voter database that discredits legitimate voters, purges of voter rolls, the 2013 Supreme Court decision striking down the heart of the Voting Rights Act, removing polling stations or cutting back polling hours, harassing people when they showed up at those stations, taking the vote away from ex-felons—the means are many, and the consequences are that a lot of people have been denied their rights, so much so that it's the other new Jim Crow. (There is no clear tally of how many voters are missing, and it's also complicated by the fact that some populations—more than six million Americans with felony convictions, for example—are prevented outright from voting, whereas others face obstacles and harassment—via voter ID laws, for example—that thin out their numbers.)

Politics is how we tell the stories we live by: how we decide if we value the health and well-being of children, or not; the autonomy of women's bodies and equality of our lives, or not; if we protect the Dreamers who came here as small children, or not; if we act on climate change, or not. Voting is far from the only way, but is a key way we shape the national narrative. We choose a story about who and what matters; we act on that story to rearrange the world around it—and then there are tax cuts to billionaires and children kicked off health care, or there are climate agreements and millions of acres of federal land protected and support for universities. We live inside what, during postmodernism's heyday, we'd call master narratives—so there's always a question of who's telling the story, who is in charge of the narrative, and what happens if that changes.

Sometimes, when journalists like Ari Berman at *Mother Jones*—the best voice on this issue—write about the suppression of the votes, people assume they're saying Hillary Clinton should have won the last presidential election. If you changed who had access to the ballot in 2016, that might have been the outcome, but the story is so much bigger than that, and the potential outcomes are so much more radical.

The Republican Party has maintained a toehold on national power by systematically, strategically, increasingly suppressing the votes of people of color over decades. They are a minority party. They could never win a fair national election with their current platform of white grievance and misogyny and favors for the most powerful, so they've set about to have unfair elections. And they have also gerrymandered the daylights out of a lot of states in order to hang onto majorities at the state and national levels; in 2012, for example, they took the majority of seats in the lower house of Congress with a minority of overall votes.

Imagine that those 20 million votes were not suppressed, that voting was made easily accessible and encouraged, rather than the opposite. The party of white grievance would be defunct or unrecognizably different from what it is today. But the Democratic Party would be different, too. Imagine that the Democratic Party had to answer to more young people, more poor people, more nonwhite people, more people who believe in strengthening human rights and social service safety nets, economic justice, stronger action on climate change. Imagine a country where Democrats weren't competing for moderate-to-conservative voters because the general electorate was far more progressive—as it would be, if all those people who lost their voting rights actually had them (and, yeah, if more younger people showed up). It wouldn't change something as small as the outcome of the 2016 election. It would mean different political parties with different platforms and different candidates, different news coverage, different outcomes. It would change the story. It would change who gets to tell the story and how all our stories get told.

We are a country that is increasingly nonwhite, and nonwhite voters are, overall, more committed to social, economic, and environmental justice. I believe that we are a country full of generous-minded progressive people, the people who voted in eight trans candidates in the November 2017 elections; and who, shortly thereafter, in the race to fill Jeff Sessions's Senate seat, voted in moderate Democrat Doug Jones over lunatic-right Republican Roy Moore in Alabama. A friend noted that without suppression of the Black vote,

Jones would have won not by less than two points but by several points. But had those votes not been suppressed one way or another since, basically, the Fifteenth Amendment gave Black men the right to vote in 1870 and the Nineteenth gave all women that right in 1920, who's to say that two white men, Moore and Jones, would have been voters' only choices, or that Alabama would be what it is today?

Teen Vogue's Sarah Mucha reported, "Deuel Ross, an attorney for the NAACP Legal Defense & Education Fund ... estimates that 118,000 registered voters in Alabama were unable to vote in [the December 17, 2017, special] election because they do not possess the proper photo identification required by Alabama law." That's about 10 percent of the vote. The game was changed by their absence, as it was by the enforced absence in 2016 of huge numbers of legitimate voters in states such as Wisconsin (one study estimated that about 200,000 more voters would have participated in Wisconsin's election, had voting conditions in 2016 been what they were as recently as 2012). It was widely noted that Black Alabamans struggled heroically to overcome the obstacles against their participation, but they should not have to.

There is good work being done, mostly on a state-by-state level, by grassroots groups and civil rights organizations, but it should be far more visible, far more passionately talked about, far more present in our imaginations. Reenfranchising the missing should be one of the great struggles of our moment. We should do it on principle, because it's about righting a grave injustice. We should also do it because these voters are, overall, people with beautiful dreams of justice, inclusion, equality, and because these voters will write a different story of what the United States of America is, and can be, and should be. A different story of who and what matters.

When you change your trajectory by even a few degrees at the outset, it can take you someplace completely different by the time you've walked a few miles, let alone gone along for decades, or a century and a half. Stripping citizens of their voting rights has steadily pushed us to the right, and we have ended up someplace we should never have been. Many lives have been crushed along the way, voices have been suppressed, wars have broken out, the urgent crisis of climate change has been denied and neglected. We can't undo what has been. The story has been told, the line has been walked. But we can correct course. We can start by telling a story that millions of missing votes matter and by working to get those voters back in the game.

II.
American Emotions

The Ideology of Isolation

(2016)

If you boil the strange soup of contemporary right-wing ideology down to a sort of bouillon cube, you find the idea that things are not connected to other things, that people are not connected to other people, and that they are all better off unconnected. The core values are individual freedom and individual responsibility: yourself for yourself, on your own. Out of this Glorious Disconnect comes all sorts of illogical thinking. Taken to its conclusion, this worldview dictates that even facts are freestanding items that the self-made man can manufacture for use as he sees fit.

This is the modern ideology we still call conservative, though it is really a sort of loopy libertarianism that inverts some of the milder propositions of earlier conservative thinkers. "There is no such thing as society," Margaret Thatcher said in an interview in 1987. The rest of her famous remark is less frequently quoted: "There is [a] living tapestry of men and women and people and the beauty of that tapestry and the quality of our lives will depend upon how much each of us is prepared to take responsibility for ourselves and each of us prepared to turn round and help by our own efforts those who are unfortunate."

Throughout that interview with *Woman's Own* magazine, Thatcher walked the line between old-school conservatism—we are all connected in a delicate tapestry that too much government meddling might tear—and the newer version: "Too many children and people have been given to understand 'I have a problem, it's the government's job to cope with it.'" At some point in the decades since, the balance tipped definitively from "government aid should not replace social connections" to "to hell with others and their problems." Or, as the cowboy sings to the calf, "It's your misfortune / And none of my own."

The cowboy is the American embodiment of this ideology of isolation, though the archetype of the self-reliant individual—like the contemporary right-wing obsession with guns—has its roots less in actual American history than in the imagined history of Cold War–era Westerns. The American West was indigenous land given to settlers by the US government and cleared for them by the US Army, crisscrossed by government-subsidized railroads and full of water projects and other enormous cooperative enterprises. All this had very little to do with Shane and the sheriff in *High Noon* or the Man with No Name in Sergio Leone's spaghetti Western trilogy. But never mind that, because a cowboy silhouetted against a sunset looks so good, whether he's Ronald Reagan or the Marlboro Man. The loner taketh not, nor does he give; he scorneth the social and relies on himself alone.

*Him*self. Women, in this mode of thinking, are too interactive in their tendency to gather and ally rather than fight or flee, and in their fluid boundaries. In fact, what is sometimes regarded as an inconsistency in the contemporary right-wing platform—the desire to regulate women's reproductive activity in particular, and sexuality in general, while deregulating everything else—is only inconsistent if you regard women as people. If you regard women as an undifferentiated part of nature, their bodies are just another place a man has every right to go.

US Supreme Court justice Clarence Thomas's first public questions, after a decade of silence during oral arguments at the Supreme Court, came in late February 2016, when he took an intense interest in whether barring people convicted of misdemeanor domestic violence from owning guns violated their constitutional rights. That there is a constitutional right for individuals to own guns is a consequence of Antonin Scalia's radically revisionist interpretation of the Second Amendment, and it's propped up on the cowboy ethos, in which guns are incredibly useful for defending oneself from bad guys and one's right to send out bullets trumps the right of others not to receive them. Facts demonstrate that very few people in this country successfully use guns to defend themselves from "bad people"—unless you count the nearly two-thirds of US gun deaths by suicide as a sad and peculiar form of self-defense. The ideologues of isolation aren't interested in those facts, or in the fact that the majority of women murdered by intimate partners in the United States are killed with guns.

But I was talking about cowboys. In *West of Everything*, Jane Tompkins describes how Westerns valued deeds over words, a tight-lipped version of masculinity over communicative femininity, and concludes: "Not speaking demonstrates control not only over feelings but over one's physical boundaries as well. The male ... maintains the integrity of the boundary that divides him from the world. (It is fitting that in the Western the ultimate loss of that control takes place when one man puts holes in another man's body.)" Fear of penetration and the fantasy of impenetrable isolation are central to both homophobia and the xenophobic mania for "sealing the border." In other words, isolation is good, freedom is disconnection, and good fences, especially on the US–Mexico border, make good neighbors.

Both Mitt Romney and Donald Trump have marketed themselves as self-made men, as lone cowboys out on the prairie of the free market, though both were born rich. Romney, in a clandestinely videotaped talk to his wealthy donors in 2012, disparaged people "who are dependent upon government, who believe that they are victims, who believe that government has a responsibility to care for them, who believe that they are entitled to health care, to food, to housing, to you name it."

Taxes represent civic connection: what we each give to the collective good. This particular form of shared interest has been framed as a form of oppression at least since Ronald Reagan, in his first inaugural address, bemoaned a "tax system which penalizes successful achievement." The spread of this right-wing hatred of taxes has been helped along by the pretense that tax revenues go to loafers and welfare queens, who offend the conservative idea of independence, rather than to things conservatives like (notably, a military that dwarfs all others) or systems that everyone needs (notably, roads and bridges).

I ran into this hatred for dependency in an online discussion of the police killing of Luis Góngora Pat, a homeless man, in San Francisco in 2016. More than a hundred messages into a fairly civil discourse started by a witness to the shooting, a commenter erupted: "I'm sick of people like you that think homeless people who can't take care of themselves and their families [and] have left them for us taxpaying citizens to care for think they have freedom. Once you can't take care of or support yourself, and expect others to carry your burden, you have lost freedom. Wake up." The same commenter later elaborated, "Have you ever owed money? Freedom lost. You owe someone. It's called personal responsibility."

Everyone on that neighborhood forum, including the writer, likely owed rent to a landlord or mortgage payments to a bank, making them more indebted than the homeless in their tents. If you're housed in any American city, you also benefit from a host of services, such as water and sanitation, and the organizations overseeing them, as well as from traffic lights and transit rules and building codes—the kind of stuff taxes pay for. But if you forget what you derive from the collective, you can imagine that you owe it nothing and can go it alone.

All this would have made that commenter's tirade incoherent, if its points weren't so familiar. This is the rhetoric of modern conservatives: freedom is a luxury that wealth affords you; wealth comes from work; those who don't work, never mind the cause, are undeserving (those who are both wealthy and don't work escape the analysis). If freedom and independence are the ideal, dependence is not merely disdained; it's furiously loathed. In her novelistic paean to free enterprise *Atlas Shrugged*, Ayn Rand called dependents parasites and looters. "We don't want to turn the safety net into a hammock that lulls able-bodied people to lives of dependency and complacency," said one of Rand's admirers, congressman Paul Ryan.

The modern right may wish that every man were an island, entire of himself, but no one is wholly independent. You can't survive without taking air into your lungs, you didn't give birth to or raise yourself, you won't bury yourself, and in between you won't produce most of the goods and services you depend on to live. Your gut is full of microorganisms without which you could not digest all the plants and animals, likely grown by other people, which you devour to survive. We are nodes on intricate systems, synapses snapping on a great collective brain; we are in it together, for better or worse.

There is, of course, such a thing as society, and you're inside it. Beyond that, beneath it and above and around and within it and us, there is such a thing as ecology, the systems within which our society exists, and with which it often clashes. Ecological thinking articulates the interdependence and interconnectedness of all things. This can be a beautiful dream of symbiosis when you're talking about how, say, a particular species of yucca depends on a particular moth to pollinate it, and how the larvae of that moth depend on the seeds of that yucca for their first meals. Or it can be a nightmare when it comes to how toxic polychlorinated biphenyls found their way to the Arctic, where they concentrated in human breast milk and in top-of-the-food-chain carnivores such as polar bears. John Muir, wandering in the Yosemite in 1869, put it this way: "When we try to pick out anything by itself, we find it hitched to everything else in the Universe."[1]

This traditional worldview could be seen as mystical or spiritual, but the accuracy of its description of natural systems within what we now call the biosphere is borne out by modern science. If you kill off the wolves in Yellowstone, elk populations will explode and many other plant and animal species will suffer; if you spray DDT on crops, it kills off pests as intended, but it will also, as Rachel Carson told us in 1962, kill the birds who would otherwise keep many insects and rodents in check.

All this causes great trouble for the ideology of isolation. It interferes with the right to maximum individual freedom, a freedom not to be bothered by others' needs. Which is why modern conservatives so insistently deny the realities of ecological interconnectedness, refusing to recognize that when you add something to or remove an element from an environment, you alter the whole in ways that may come back to bite you. The usual argument in defense of this pesticide or that oil platform is that it is an isolated element rather than part of a far-reaching system, and sometimes—increasingly, nowadays—that this far-reaching system does not even exist.

No problem more clearly demonstrates the folly of individualist thinking—or more clearly calls for a systematic response—than

---

1. Muir did not acknowledge Native Americans as a crucial presence in the landscape in which he had that epiphany, a troubling erasure that's central to the thesis of my 1994 book *Savage Dreams*.

climate change. The ideologues of isolation are doubly challenged by this fact. They reject the proposed solutions to climate change, because they bristle at the need for limits on production and consumption, for regulation, for cooperation between industry and government, and for international partnership. In 2011 Naomi Klein attended a meeting at the Heartland Institute, a libertarian think tank, and produced a landmark essay about why conservatives are so furiously opposed to doing anything about climate change. She quotes a man from the Competitive Enterprise Institute, who declared, "No free society would do to itself what this agenda requires…. The first step to that is to remove these nagging freedoms that keep getting in the way." Klein reported, "Most of all, however, I will hear versions of the opinion expressed by the county commissioner in the fourth row: that climate change is a Trojan horse designed to abolish capitalism and replace it with some kind of eco-socialism."

On a more fundamental level, the very *idea* of climate change is offensive to isolationists because it tells us more powerfully and urgently than anything ever has that everything is connected, that nothing exists in isolation. What comes out of your tailpipe or your smokestack or your leaky fracking site contributes to the changing mix of the atmosphere, where increasing quantities of carbon dioxide and other greenhouse gases cause the earth to retain more of the heat that comes from the sun, which doesn't just result in what we used to call global warming but will lead to climate chaos.

As the fact of climate change has become more and more difficult to deny, the ideologues of isolation deny instead our responsibility for the problem and the possibility that we are capable of acting collectively to do anything about it. "Climate change occurs no matter what," Paul Ryan said a few years ago. "The question is, can and should the federal government do something about it? And

I would argue the federal government, with all its tax and regulatory schemes, can't." Of course it can, but he prefers that it not do so, which is why he denies human impact as a cause and human solutions as a treatment.

What keeps the ideology of isolation going is going to extremes. If you begin by denying social and ecological systems, then you end by denying the reality of facts, which are, after all, part of a network of systematic relationships among language, physical reality, and the record, regulated by the rules of evidence, truth, grammar, word meaning, and so forth. You deny the relationship between cause and effect, evidence and conclusion; or, rather, you imagine both as products on the free market that one can produce and consume according to one's preferences. You deregulate meaning.

Absolute freedom means you can have any truth you like—and isolation's ideologues like truths that keep free market fundamentalism going. You can be like that unnamed senior adviser (probably Karl Rove), who, in a mad moment of Bush-era triumphalism, told Ron Suskind in 2004, "We're an empire now, and when we act, we create our own reality." Reality, in this worldview, is a product, subject to market rules or military rules, and if you are dominant in the marketplace or rule the empire, your reality can push aside the other options. "Freedom" is just another word for nothing left to limit your options. And this is how the ideology of isolation becomes nihilism, trying to kill the planet and most living things on it with a confidence born of total disconnection.

Naïve Cynicism

(2016)

On April 24, 1916—Easter Monday—Irish republicans in Dublin and a handful of other places across Ireland staged an armed rebellion against British occupation. At the time, the British Empire was the greatest power on earth; Ireland was its oldest and nearest colony. That the puny colony might oust the giant seemed farfetched, and by most measures the endeavor was a failure. The leaders were executed; the British occupation continued. But not for long: the Easter Uprising is now generally understood as a crucial step in a process that led, in 1937, to full independence for most of the island. More than a hundred years on, some view the uprising of 1916 as the beginning of the end of the British Empire.

It seems to be taken for granted that the Arab Spring uprisings, too, were a failure, since conditions in many of the affected countries are now just different kinds of dire than they were before. But the public display of a passionate desire for participatory government, the demonstration of the strength of popular power and the weakness of despotic regimes, and the sheer (if short-lived) exhilaration that took place in 2011 may have sown seeds that have not yet germinated.

I am not arguing for overlooking the violence and instability that are now plaguing North Africa and the Middle East. Nor am I optimistic about the near future of the region. I do not know what the long-term consequences of the Arab Spring will be, and neither does anyone else. We live in a time when the news media and other purveyors of conventional wisdom like to report on the future more than on the past. They draw on polls and false analogies to announce what is going to happen next, and their frequent errors— about the unelectability of a Black presidential candidate, say, or the inevitability of this or that oil pipeline—don't seem to impede their habit of prophecy or our willingness to abide them. "We don't actually know" is their least favorite thing to report.

Non-pundits, too, use bad data and worse analysis to pronounce with great certainty on future inevitabilities, present impossibilities, and past failures. The mind-set behind these statements is what I call naïve cynicism. It bleeds the sense of possibility and maybe the sense of responsibility out of people.

Cynicism is, first of all, a style of presenting oneself, and more than anything cynics take pride in not being fooled and not being foolish. But in the forms in which I encounter it, cynicism is frequently both these things. That the attitude priding itself on world-weary experience is often so naïve says much about the triumph of style over substance, attitude over analysis.

Maybe it also says something about the tendency to oversimplify. If simplification means reducing things to their essentials, oversimplification tosses aside the essential as well. It is a relentless pursuit of certainty and clarity in a world that generally offers neither, a desire to shove nuances and complexities into clear-cut binaries. Naïve cynicism concerns me because it flattens out the past and the future, and because it reduces the motivation to participate in public life, public discourse, and even intelligent conversation that distinguishes shades of gray, ambiguities and ambivalences, uncertainties, unknowns, and opportunities. Instead, we conduct our conversations like wars, and the heavy artillery of grim confidence is the weapon many reach for.

Naïve cynics shoot down possibilities, including the possibility of exploring the full complexity of any situation. They take aim at the less cynical, so that cynicism becomes a defensive posture and an avoidance of dissent. They recruit through brutality. If you set purity and perfection as your goals, you have an almost foolproof system according to which everything will necessarily fall short. But expecting perfection is naïve; failing to perceive value by using an impossible standard of measure is even more so. Cynics are often disappointed idealists and upholders of unrealistic standards. They are uncomfortable with victories, because victories are almost always temporary, incomplete, and compromised—but also because the openness of hope is dangerous, and in war, self-defense comes first. Naïve cynicism is absolutist; its practitioners assume that anything you don't deplore, you wholeheartedly endorse. But denouncing anything less than perfection as morally compromising means pursuing aggrandizement of the self, not engagement with a place or system or community, as the highest priority.

Different factions have different versions of naïve cynicism. For example, the mainstream discounts political action that proceeds outside the usual corridors of power. When Occupy Wall Street began several years ago, the movement was mocked, dismissed, and willfully misunderstood before it was hastily pronounced dead. Its obituary has been written dozens of times over the years by people who'd prefer that the rabble who blur the lines between the homeless and the merely furious not have a political role to play.

But the fruits of Occupy are too many to count. People who were involved with local encampments tell me that their thriving offshoots are still making a difference. California alone was said to have more than 140 Occupy groups; what each of them did is impossible to measure. There were results as direct as homeless advocacy, as indirect as a shift in the national debates about housing, medical and student debt, economic injustice, and inequality. There has also been effective concrete action—from debt strikes to state legislation—on these issues. Occupy helped to bring politicians such as Bernie Sanders, Bill de Blasio, and Elizabeth Warren into the mainstream.

The inability to concretely assess what Occupy accomplished comes in part from the assumption that historical events either produce straightforward, quantifiable, immediate results or they fail to matter. It's as though we're talking about bowling: either that ball knocked over those pins in that lane or it didn't. But historical forces are not bowling balls. If they were, to pursue the metaphor, bowling would be some kind of metaphysical game, shrouded in mists and unfolding over decades. The ball might knock over one pin and then another one fifteen years later, and possibly roll a strike in some other lane that most of us had forgotten even existed, and those pins would have children or spiritual heirs, and so it would go, unfolding out of sight and beyond our capacity to predict. That's sort of what the Easter Uprising did, and what Occupy and Black Lives Matter are doing now.

Like mainstream naïve cynics, those on the margins and to the left also doubt their own capacity to help bring about change, a view that conveniently spares them the hard work such change requires. I recently shared on social media a passage from an issue of *Nature Climate Change*, in which a group of scientists outlined the impact of climate change over the next ten thousand years. Their portrait is terrifying, but it is not despairing: "This long-term view shows that the next few decades offer a brief window of opportunity to minimize large-scale and potentially catastrophic climate change that will extend longer than the entire history of human civilization thus far." That's a sentence about catastrophe but also about opportunity. The first comment I received was, "There's nothing that's going to stop the consequences of what we have already done/not done." This was another way of saying, "I'm pitting my own casual assessment over peer-reviewed science; I'm not reading carefully; I'm making a thwacking sound with my false omniscience." Such comments represent a reflex response that can be used to meet wildly different stimuli. Naïve cynicism remains obdurate in the face of varied events, some of which are positive, some negative, some mixed, and quite a lot of them unfinished.

The climate movement has grown powerful and diverse. In North America it is shutting down coal plants and preventing new ones from being built. It has blocked fracking, oil and gas leases on public land, drilling in the Arctic, pipelines, and oil trains that carry the stuff that would otherwise run through the thwarted pipelines. Forty-seven US cities and towns and the state of Hawaii have committed to going 100 percent renewable in the near future; five cities have already met that goal.

Remarkable legislation has been introduced even on the national level, such as bills in both the House and the Senate to bar new fossil-fuel extraction on public lands. Those bills will almost certainly not pass in the current Congress, but they introduce to the mainstream a position that was inconceivable a few years ago. This is how epochal change often begins, with efforts that fail in their direct aims but succeed in shifting the conversation and opening space for further action. These campaigns and achievements are far from enough; they need to scale up, and scaling up means drawing in people who recognize that there are indeed opportunities worth seizing.

Late in 2015, some key federal decisions to curtail drilling for oil in the Arctic and to prevent the construction of a tar-sands pipeline were announced. The naïvely cynical dismissed them as purely a consequence of the plummeting price of oil. Activism had nothing to do with it, I was repeatedly told. But had there been no activism, the Arctic would have been drilled, and the pipelines to get the dirty crude cheaply out of Alberta built, before the price drop. It wasn't either/or; it was both.

David Roberts, a climate journalist for *Vox*, notes that the disparagement of the campaign to stop the Keystone XL pipeline assumed that activists' only goal was to prevent this one pipeline from being built, and that since this one pipeline's cancellation wouldn't save the world, the effort was futile. Roberts named these armchair quarterbacks of climate action the Doing It Wrong Brigade. He compared their critique to "criticizing the Montgomery bus boycott because it only affected a relative handful of blacks. The point of civil rights campaigns was not to free black people from discriminatory systems one at a time. It was to change the culture."

The Keystone fight was a transnational education in tar-sands and pipeline politics, as well as in the larger dimensions of climate issues. It was a successful part of a campaign to wake people up and make them engage with the terrifying stakes in this conflict. It changed the culture.

Similarly, the decision by Congress in December 2015 to allow crude oil to be exported was widely excoriated, and it was indeed a bad thing. But many commenters ignored the fact that it was part of a quid pro quo that extended tax credits for solar and wind power. Those who have studied the matter closely, such as Michael Levi and Varun Sivaram at the Council on Foreign Relations, believe that this extension "will do far more to reduce carbon dioxide emissions over the next five years than lifting the export ban will do to increase them."

Accommodating change and uncertainty requires a looser sense of self, an ability to respond in various ways. This is perhaps why qualified success unsettles those who are locked into fixed positions. The shift back to failure is a defensive measure. It is, in the end, a technique for turning away from the always imperfect, often important victories that life on Earth provides—and for lumping things together regardless of scale. If corruption is evenly distributed and ubiquitous, then there is no adequate response—or, rather, no response is required. This is so common an attitude that Bill McKibben launched a preemptive strike against it when he first wrote about the revelations that Exxon knew about climate change as early as the 1970s: "A few observers, especially on the professionally jaded left, have treated the story as old news—as something that even if we didn't know, we knew. 'Of course, they lied,' someone told me. That cynicism, however, serves as the most effective kind of cover for Exxon."

Even so, in response to the Exxon news, I heard many say airily, "Oh, all corporations lie." But the revelations were indeed news. The scale is different from any corrupt and dishonest thing a corporation has ever done, and it's important to appreciate the difference. The dismissive "It's all corrupt" line of reasoning pretends to excoriate what it ultimately excuses.

When a corporation writes something off, it accepts the cost. When we write off corporations as inherently corrupt, we accept the cost, too. Doing so paves the way for passivity and defeat. The superb and uncynical journalists at the *Los Angeles Times* and *Inside Climate News* who exposed Exxon, along with the activists who pushed on the issue, prompted the attorneys general of New York and California to launch investigations that became the basis for lawsuits against the company. And the revelations offer us opportunities to respond—in David Roberts's terms, to change the culture.

Like the tactics used by the much-disparaged fossil-fuel-divest-ment movement, the Exxon exposés have delegitimized a major power in ways that can have far-reaching consequences.

What is the alternative to naïve cynicism? An active response to what arises, a recognition that we often don't know what is going to happen ahead of time, and an acceptance that whatever takes place will usually be a mixture of blessings and curses that will unfold over considerable time. Such an attitude is bolstered by historical memory, by accounts of indirect consequences, unanticipated cata-clysms and victories, cumulative effects, and long timelines.

Naïve cynicism loves itself more than the world; it defends itself in lieu of defending the world. I'm interested in the people who love the world more, and in what they have to tell us, which varies from day to day, subject to subject. Because what we do begins with what we believe we can do. It begins with being open to the possibilities and interested in the complexities.

Facing the Furies

(2017)

In 1979, a catchy Kenny Rogers song called "Coward of the County" made it to the top of the country charts. It's about a man named Tommy, whose father, a prisoner, implores him not to follow the example he's been set:

> *Promise me, son, not to do the things I've done*
> *Walk away from trouble if you can*
> *Now, it won't mean you're weak if you turn the other cheek*

This is early modern country music, so the song takes for granted that you've got to honor thy father, but it is also committed to the eye-for-an-eye ethos of the Old Testament: when Tommy's girlfriend is gang-raped, the paternal instructions fall by the wayside. The former coward of the county beats the hell out of the perpetrators. Only violence can redeem his reputation, and his reputation is indistinguishable from his manhood—Tommy's masculinity, not recompense for his lover, is what is really at stake in this story. Turning the other cheek, we learn, is weak after all.

"Coward of the County" celebrates rage as an affirmation of the self and of one's virility. It poses a question to which the right answer is violence. Nine years after the song came out, the same question was posed to Democratic candidate Michael Dukakis during his campaign for president. Would he, if his wife were raped and murdered, favor the death penalty for her attacker? The candidate's answer—"I think there are better and more effective ways to deal with violent crime"—was widely considered to have sunk his campaign. A lack of vengeful bloodlust made him not a model of self-restraint or mercy but the coward of the country.

The philosopher Martha Nussbaum calls the path Dukakis repudiated "the road of payback." The urge to exact revenge, she argues, derives from our desire for "cosmic balance," as well as our attempts to overcome helplessness through displays of power. By this logic, revenge rights the scales, despite doing nothing to restore what was lost or repair what was damaged.

Sometimes there are good reasons for a strong response, including the prevention of further harm. But more often, lashing out is a way to avoid looking inward. A 2001 study by Jennifer Lerner and Dacher Keltner found that feeling angry made people as optimistic about the outcome of a situation as feeling happy. In other words, anger may make people miserable, but it also makes them more confident and crowds out other, more introspective miseries: pain, fear, guilt, uncertainty, vulnerability. We'd rather be mad than sad.

In our political conversations, anger is constantly invoked yet rarely examined. What exactly is it? At its most basic, it is a physiological reaction to threat, one we share with other mammals. Anger manifests as a collection of somatic responses—accelerated heart rate, increased blood pressure, heightened body temperature—that are associated with alertness, focus, readiness to act. But the similarity to other animals ends there. Where a dog may growl, bristle, or bite you if you poke it with a stick, it will have no such reaction if you insult its god or its sports team or talk about someone you know who poked another dog. In fact, a good deal of clickbait journalism amounts to stories about someone, some-where, poking another dog; our taste for indignation is a leash eas-ily yanked.

For our species, with its imaginative and narrative capacities, challenges to one's status, beliefs, and advantages also register as threats. Human anger is a response to insecurity both literal and imagined, to any sense that our physical or social or emotional wel-fare is at risk. Attacks of fury can bring on strokes and heart attacks and blood clots. We routinely die of rage.

At its mildest, the emotion is no more than annoyance, an aversion to minor unpleasantness. Annoyance with an ethical character becomes indignation: not only do I dislike that, but it also should not have happened. Indeed, anger generally arises from a sense of being wronged. In this respect, my conviction that you should not have eaten the last slice resembles my conviction that we should not have bombed Iraq: in each case, I see an injustice and wish it to be righted. Anger that is motivated by more than a mammalian instinct for self-protection operates by an ethic, a sense of how things ought or ought not to be. But the sentiment's ethical component doesn't explain its psychological effects. Anger is hostile to understanding. At its most implacable or extreme, it prevents comprehension of a situation, of the people you oppose, of your own role and responsibilities. It's not for nothing that we call rages "blind."

Is anyone more possessed by this kind of obliterating anger than Donald Trump? Our nation is currently led by a petty, vindic-tive, histrionic man whose exceptional privilege has robbed him of even the most rudimentary training in dealing with setbacks and slights. He was elected by people who were drawn to him because he homed in on their anger, made them even angrier, and promised vengeance on the usual targets, domestic and foreign, successfully clouding their judgment as to what electing him would mean for their health care, safety, environment, education, economy.

Yet Trump's furious ascent is only the culmination of fury's long journey toward enshrinement in this country. Our legal system, for example, has been lurching backward for some time from the ideal of impartial justice toward a model based on retaliation. The prison system still employs a plethora of terms that suggest otherwise—"rehabilitation," "reform," "correction," and the penitence implicit in penitentiaries—but its current rhetoric and practices are often purely punitive. Families of crime victims are now sometimes invited to the executions of their relatives' attackers, as though the death penalty were an instrument of personal revenge. (Many of those families decline to participate, and some have protested the sentences.)

Governments regularly manufacture or exaggerate threats to suggest that violence is necessary and restraint would constitute weakness: during World War II, the United States condemned citizens of Japanese heritage; during the postwar period, it targeted leftists. After the collapse of the Soviet Union, it scrambled to find new adversaries, and has since settled on Muslims, immigrants, and transgender people. The provocation of anger is essential to government by manipulation, and the angriest people are often the most credulous, willing to snatch up without scrutiny whatever feeds their fire.

On social media, audiences give perfunctory attention to facts so that they can move on to the pleasure of righteous wrath about the latest person who has said or done something wrong. Anger is the stock-in-trade of many politicians and pundits and of the tabloids and websites that give them voice; it is the go-to emotion, perhaps because it is inherently reactive, volatile—easy to provoke, easy to direct. Indeed, as Jeffrey M. Berry and Sarah Sobieraj argue in *The Outrage Industry*, it has become a kind of commodity, a product target-marketed to specific audiences. Anger-provoking content is more likely to succeed, more likely to "stick," not least because anger itself is a way the mind gets stuck.

Many of the more prominent media outlets trafficking in outrage—making ad hominem attacks, dividing the political world into heroes and villains, giving us this day our daily rage—are aimed at conservatives: Fox News, say, or the talk radio networks. But many on the left are equally smitten with anger. I grew up in the shadow of the slogan "If you're not angry, you're not paying attention," which equates the feeling with engagement, with principles; it suggests that you cannot have the latter without the former. Righteous rage is often seen as a virtue.

Rage is not quite the same thing as outrage. You might say that the latter is motivated less by wrath at what has been done than by empathy for those it has been done to. People showed up to the huge demonstration at the San Francisco airport on January 28, 2017, when the ban on travelers from majority-Muslim countries went into effect, not to harm anyone but to prevent others from being harmed. And yet when it comes to motivations, the distinction between love and hate is not as easy to delineate as it might seem. It's rare that anyone admits to a desire to hurt. The antiabortion movement invokes love for unborn children as justification for its actions, but to nearly everyone else it appears driven mostly by resentment of women's autonomy. That wrath has led to some of the most deadly domestic terrorism in this country.

Most committed activists are motivated by love, though love and hate can blur: one can claim to hate on the grounds that one's hate is against what menaces what one loves. Robert Lewis Dear, Jr., who claimed to be "a warrior for the babies," shot and killed three parents of young children at the Colorado Springs Planned Parenthood (Providing abortions is 3 percent of Planned Parenthood's work; 80 percent of its services are to prevent the unintended pregnancies that sometimes lead to abortions.) Some start out with love and make the long journey to hate unintentionally. Anger is not hate, but when the desire to harm that it can arouse settles on a designated target—that's hate.

In part because hate is so often mistaken for love in these conflicts, it's dangerous to grant anger a special authenticity. The ire of conservative voters is regularly regarded as a deep augury of real concerns, real convictions, even as the ease with which crowds can be incited—and the weak (or nonexistent) factual basis for many of their concerns—is demonstrated again and again. People at all points on the political spectrum are often furious about things they had not previously paid much attention to and don't know much about. Anger is frequently mistaken for a dowsing rod indicating something deep, when it is better understood as a dial that can be spun with a flick of the finger.

Who has the right to be angry? Anger is considered justified if it is a reaction to outrageous circumstance, so denying the grounds for anger denies its legitimacy. And behind the question of who has the right to be angry is the question of who is allowed to act on anger. Denying the reality of racism's impact is an essential part of demonizing the anger of nonwhite people as unreasonable, baseless, even criminal. And when women are angry, it's seen as a character flaw. For decades people have stereotyped feminists as angry, and in doing so have denied aspects of women's experiences that it is reasonable to be angry about (and that feminist women might, in fact, be sad about, or weary of, or full of empathy for those who suffer from), but all negative women's emotion is seen as anger, and all anger as a failing). Black women get it twice, their anger delegitimized by reasons of race and of gender.

In the conservative Christian culture in which the writer Kelly Sundberg grew up, forgiveness was considered an essential feminine virtue. Praising it in girls and women, she notes, encouraged them to excuse men's transgressions—beatings, betrayals—again and again. The imperative to forgive made a virtue of powerlessness. Women's and people of color's relationships to power will remain uneasy as long as the right to be angry is seen as a white male prerogative. There are a few country songs—by Martina McBride, the Dixie Chicks, Carrie Underwood—that describe killing abusive spouses. But violence in "Coward of the County" makes the protagonist, Tommy, manly; in the hymns to killing your husband, no one is made more of a woman—they're just more likely to survive.

The terms used by primatologists are unsettlingly helpful to understanding the social role of anger: "threat display," "dominance behavior." Expressions of rage are a means of exercising control over others and asserting status, a status defined in part by the right to dominate, which belongs to parents, bosses, police officers, husbands. "Dominate" is what Tommy ultimately did, what Dukakis failed to do.

As Nussbaum points out, "People with an overweening sense of their own privilege … seem particularly prone to angry displays." The more you expect to get your own way, in other words, the more upset you are likely to be at being thwarted; those who are most thwarted must learn to apportion their wrath with care. Indeed, the most deeply wronged are often the least interested in resentment. In her essay "The Uses of Anger," Audre Lorde reflects that women of color "have had to learn to orchestrate those furies so that they do not tear us apart." In an obituary for Nelson Mandela, the writer Stephen Smith makes a similar point. In prison, he writes, Mandela came "to see that hatred and enmity were mimetic, a trap laid by the 'evil' other: fall into it and you and your adversary become hard to tell apart." Mandela, who was as entitled to anger as anyone, nevertheless gave it up. But he did not give up his endeavor to change the world around him. The difference is significant.

Fury is a renewable resource; though the initial anger may be fleeting, it can be revived and strengthened by telling and retelling yourself the story of the insult or injustice, even over a lifetime. Many accounts of American anger focus on what people are angry about, as though reactive anger were inevitable and the outside stimulus provoking it the only variable. They rarely discuss the status of anger or the habits of mind that support it. Those are discussed elsewhere, in spiritual and psychological literature and in anthropological texts.

In Christianity, wrath is one of the seven deadly sins; patience, a cardinal virtue, is its opposite. Buddhist theology regards anger as one of the three poisons, an affliction to be overcome through self-discipline and self-awareness. "The traditional ethical precept about anger is sometimes translated as not to get angry," Taigen Dan Leighton, a Zen priest and translator of Buddhist texts, explained to me. "But in modern Sōtō Zen Buddhism, we say not to harbor ill will." The Buddhist writer Thanissara (Mary Weinberg) put it thus: "Anger is traditionally thought to be close to wisdom. When not projected outward onto others or inward toward the self, it gives us the necessary energy and clarity to understand what needs to be done."

We will all feel anger at one time or another, but it doesn't need to become animosity or be renewed and retained. Buddhism offers an elegant model of anger management. Harness the emotion. Feel it without inflicting it.

Some cultures consider anger a luxury in which one should not indulge. The Machiguenga of the Peruvian Amazon, a 1986 study suggests, regard anger as dangerous, undesirable, and closely tied to violence. Jean Briggs, an anthropologist, lived with Inuit people in Canada in the early 1960s and reported that they highly valued emotional control: "The maintenance of equanimity under trying circumstances," she observed, "is *the* essential sign of maturity, of adulthood." Volatile adults were seen as disruptive, disturbing. Anger was something you were supposed to outgrow.

We in America have not outgrown anger; we don't even think we should. The left in particular has viewed anger as an essential catalyst for change, a belief evident in the names of demonstrations and movements. In 1969, the Weather Underground organized the Days of Rage, in which the several hundred young radicals who showed up were outnumbered and outfought by the Chicago police. Across the pond, in the 1970s, Britain's Angry Brigade carried out a series of small-scale bombings. In 1991, the political rock band Rage Against the Machine was formed, and throughout most of the 1990s the anarchist collective Love and Rage put out a newspaper of the same name.

Left-wing activists have had chronic arguments about whether petty violence—smashing things, fisticuffs, throwing rocks, not the stuff that overthrows regimes, exactly—is a useful strategy for social change. Those who argue for it often use shaming: if you don't support violence, you're cowardly, compromised, that worst of insults, liberal. But violence's defenders fall back, often, on the argument that violence is a form of individual self-expression, and no one has the right to deny others that expression.

This appears to come from an old idea: that which does not freely flow is bottled up, building up unhealthy psychic pressure. Which assumes that the urge is inevitable, the river must flow to the sea; it does not question what feeds the river, whether it inevitably flows, and what other directions its flows might take. Justified thus, violence becomes a form of personal expression, part of bourgeois individualism rather than global revolutionary strategy. One is really fighting against one's own repression rather than that of others, and devil take the consequences. This is an argument that has nothing to do with strategy or winning.[1]

We speak of blind rages; I know the last thing that made me angry—an anti-Semitic comment—got me stuck in replaying the details of the interaction, buttressing my arguments as though I would fight the charges in court, and generally simmering for thirty-six hours or so that might have been spent more profitably and pleasantly on almost anything else. The slur took place in the course of a conversation about the uses of left-wing violence. The comment, you could say, called a whole ethnic group on a whole continent the cowards of the county: "And didn't 6 million die because they didn't resist the Nazi regime?" After I questioned the remark, the speaker eventually apologized and admitted the factual inanity of his statement, but I was nevertheless stuck.

The anger crowded out other thoughts, got me mired in a moment that didn't threaten me directly (though anti-Semitic slurs, and the beliefs behind them, underlie anti-Semitic acts, which are having a resurgence right now). It was as though something weighty and hard-edged had slammed shut in my chest, and a fire simmered inside. It was as though my mind was on a treadmill revisiting the Polish partisans, the French Resistance, the Warsaw ghetto uprising, Primo Levi in the Italian Resistance, and so forth. But this rumination was not, overall, pleasant or productive, and when I finally exited the treadmill I vowed to self-regulate better.

In my experience, those dedicated to practical change over the long term are often the least involved in the dramas of rage, which wear on both the self and others. After reading or listening to, say,

---

1. All this was, of course, written before the rise of Antifa, the volunteers countering white-supremacist violence, which is a whole different story in a whole different era.

hundreds of detailed accounts of rape, you may remain deeply motivated to engage in political action but find it difficult to get indignant about the newest offense. The most committed organizers I know are not often incensed. Their first obligation is to changing how things are—to action, not self-expression.

Much political rhetoric suggests that without anger there is no powerful engagement, that anger is a sort of gasoline that runs the engine of social change. But sometimes gasoline just makes things explode.

Preaching to the Choir

(2017)

Once, on a river-rafting trip through the Grand Canyon, I traveled with a charming, good-humored man who ran an oil rig in the Gulf of Mexico. He liked to rail against Nancy Pelosi, who had recently become the Speaker of the House. One day I told him that I, too, disliked Pelosi, because she was well to my right on many issues. The man was staggered; he'd imagined that she defined the left-most rim of the universe, beyond which nothing existed.

When the oilman was on land he lived in Colorado Springs; I'm a San Franciscan. Geography alone made us exotic species to each other. The river trip came during a period in 2009 when I frequently found myself telling strangers, in frustration, that people in my hometown could be as closed-minded as in any right-wing community. We were all living in our respective bubbles; I was looking for more substantive exchange. Yet what transpired in my conversations on the raft was not, in the end, especially illuminating. I enjoyed the oilman's Texas vernacular, and we found common ground in our appreciation for buttermilk biscuits, but neither of us changed the other's mind about the fossil fuel industry, and neither tried to, which may be why the encounter seems so pleasant in recollection.

The phrase *preaching to the choir* properly means hectoring your listeners with arguments they already agree with, and it's a common sin of radicals—the tendency to upbraid others as a way of announcing one's own virtue. But it is often applied too widely, to malign and dismiss conversation between people whose beliefs more or less coincide. The phrase implies that political work should be primarily evangelical, even missionary; that the task is to go out and convert the heathens; that talking to those with whom we agree achieves nothing. But only the most patient and skillful among us can alter the views of those with whom we disagree profoundly.

And is there no purpose in getting preached to, in gathering with your compatriots? Why else do we go to church but to sing, to pray a little, to ease our souls, to see our friends, and to hear the sermon? I asked Katya Lysander, who sings ancient and modern Eastern European music with a Chicago choral group, what she thought of the phrase. She pointed out that there are in fact four audiences in a church service—the congregation, the choir, the preacher, and God. A priest preaching directly to the choir would be facing the wrong way, away from the congregation, since the choir is usually behind or on either side of the pulpit. And, as Lysander might have added, the preacher also listens to the choir, to her bishops, her colleagues, her congregation, and her sacred texts. And then everyone catches up on the church (or synagogue or mosque) steps after the service. The ecclesiastical conversation, that is to say, consists of a series of exchanges among people in many different roles.

What's more, to suggest that you shouldn't preach to the choir is to misunderstand the nature of preaching. Conversion or the transmission of new information is not the primary aim; the preacher has other work to do. Classically, the sermon is a kind of literary criticism that regards the key sacred texts and their meanings as inexhaustible. Don't many adults, like most small children, love hearing some stories more than once, and aren't there always new perspectives on the deepest ones? Most religions have prayers and narratives, hymns and songs that are seen as wells of meaning that never run dry. You can go lay down your sword and shield by the riverside one more time; there are always more ways to say how once you were blind and now can see.

Karen Haygood Stokes, a minister in Grand Rapids, Michigan, who formerly belonged to the San Francisco Symphony Choir, explained to me that her aim is not so much to persuade people to believe as it is to encourage them to inquire into existing beliefs. "My task as a preacher is to find the places of agreement and then move someplace from there. Not to change anybody's mind, but to deepen an understanding." The common ground among her parishioners is not the destination; it's the starting point: "Have we thought critically about *why* we agree?" It's a call to go deeper, to question yourself.

The primary assumption behind the idea that we shouldn't preach to the choir is that one's proper audience is one's enemies, not one's allies. This becomes especially true during election season, the prevailing view being that elections are won not by focusing on the base but by flipping the opposition. By this reasoning, all that I write and say during those cycles should be pitched at my adversaries, to recruit them. I have often been admonished that my statements should give no offense to strangers with whom I have little in common, that I should say things—I'm not sure what these cottony words would be, or whether I contain them—that will not irritate or alienate. I should spend my efforts on people who disagree passionately with me, because why waste time on those with whom I've already formed relationships and share interests?

One of the most excruciating rites of recent presidential elections is the debate in which "undecided" or swing voters are brought in to ask questions of the candidates. The premise behind the spectacle is that candidates win by competing for those not sure whether they are for or against civil rights, tax cuts for the rich, and so on. Yet much evidence suggests that political organizations benefit most from motivating those who already agree with them—by pursuing people who don't know *whether* they'll vote, rather than how they'll vote. This means reaching constituents who, historically, have been less likely to go to the polling booth: the poor, the young, the non-white. Republicans know this, which is why they've worked hard to perfect voter suppression tactics that target those populations.

Nevertheless, centrist Democrats often go wooing those who don't support them, thereby betraying those who do. It's as though you ditched not only your congregation but your credo in the hope of making inroads among believers of some other faith. You think you're recruiting; really, you're losing your religion. This has been true with welfare "reform," with the war on terror, with economic policies punishing the poor, with the fantasy of winning over "the white working class": time and again, misguided attempts to bring in new voters have betrayed existing constituencies.

In 2017, in an effort to appeal to a more conservative demographic, some Democrats went so far as to slacken their commitment to reproductive rights, dismissing them as "identity politics" and deeming them less important than economic justice. As many women have pointed out, however, such a stance constitutes a failure to understand that until and unless this half of the population can control their bodies and plan their families, they cannot be economically equal. The question is one of both strategy and principle: Do you win by chasing those who don't share your views, or by serving and respecting those already with you? Is the purpose of the choir to sing to the infidels or inspire the faithful? What happens if the faithful stop showing up, donating, doing the work?

One reason we emphasize conversion is that we tend to believe that ideas matter more than actions, that a preponderance of agreement will result in political and social change. In years past, I've often heard people obsess over polls that revealed how many Americans think climate change is real. They seemed convinced that if everyone could be convinced to believe, the crisis would be solved. But if people who already believe climate change is real and pressing do nothing to address the problem, nothing happens. Not only is it unlikely that everyone will agree, it doesn't matter whether they do, and it isn't worth waiting for. There are still people who don't believe that women are endowed with the same inalienable rights as men, and this hasn't prevented us from creating policies that are based on the principle of equality between the sexes.

What matters is that some of us act. In 2006, the political scientist Erica Chenoweth set out to determine whether nonviolence was as effective for regime change as violence. She found, to her surprise, that nonviolent strategies worked better. Organizers were enthralled by her conclusion that only around 3.5 percent of a population was needed to successfully resist or even topple a regime nonviolently. In other words, to create change, you don't need everyone to agree with you; you just need some people to agree so passionately that they will donate, campaign, march, risk arrest or injury, possibly prison or death. Their passionate conviction may influence others. Ideas originate at the margins and migrate inward to succeed; insisting that your idea must have arrived rather than be traveling is to miss how change works.

The majority of Americans, according to Gallup polls from the early 1960s, did not support the tactics of the civil rights movement, and less than a quarter of the public approved of the 1963 March on Washington. Nevertheless, the march helped push the federal government to pass the 1964 Civil Rights Act. It was at the march that Martin Luther King Jr. gave his "I Have a Dream" speech—an example of preaching to the choir at its best. King spoke to inspire his supporters rather than persuade his detractors. He disparaged moderation and gradualism; he argued that his listeners' dissatisfaction was legitimate and necessary, that they must demand drastic change. White allies were needed, but Black activists didn't need to wait for them. Often, it's an example of passionate idealism that converts others. The performance of integrity is more influential than that of compromise. Sometimes, rather than meeting people where they are, you can locate yourself someplace they will eventually want to be.

The choir is made up of the deeply committed: those who show up every Sunday, listen to every sermon, and tithe like crazy. The time the choristers spend with one another, the sum of their sympathy and shared experience, is part of what helps them sing in unison and in tune. To win politically, you need to motivate your own.

The pursuit of insight also gets dismissed as preaching to the choir. There are a thousand things beyond the fact of blunt agreement that you might need or want to discuss with your friends and allies and colleagues. There are strategy and practical management, the finer points of a theory, values and goals both incremental and ultimate, reassessment as things change for better or worse. Effective speech in this model isn't alchemy; it doesn't transform what people believe. It's electricity: it galvanizes them to act. Or it helps them know why something matters or where they stand.

I wonder if I hear the phrase *preaching to the choir* often now because we have, in our everyday practices, pared our communications down to the bone and beyond. Almost no one I know calls friends merely to have the kind of long, reflective, intimate conversations that were common in earlier decades; phones are for practical exchanges—renegotiating plans, checking in on arrangements. Emails, which in the 1990s seemed to resemble letters, now resemble texting, brief bursts of words in a small space, not to be composed as art, archived, or mused over much. A lot of people are too busy to hang out without a clear purpose, or don't know that you can, and the often combative arenas and abstracted contact of social media replace physical places (including churches) to hang out in person.

Correspondence, that beautiful word, describes both an exchange of letters and the existence of affinities; we correspond because we correspond. As a young woman, I had long, intense conversations with other young women about difficult mothers, unreliable men, about heartaches and ambitions and anxieties. Sometimes these conversations were circular; sometimes they got bogged down by our inability to accept that we weren't going to get what seemed right or fair. But at their best, they reinforced that our perceptions and emotions were not baseless or illegitimate, that others were on our side and shared our experiences, that we had value and possibility. We were strengthening ourselves and our ties to one another.

Conversation is a principal way that we convey our support and love to each other; it's how we find out who our friends are and often how friendship takes place. A friendship could be imagined as an ongoing conversation, and a conversation as a collaboration of minds, and that collaboration as a brick out of which a culture or a community is built. The term *preaching to the choir* dismisses both the emotional and intellectual value of talk.

In an ideal intellectual exchange, disagreement doesn't mean tearing down a rival but testing and strengthening the structure of a proposal, an analysis. It is what you do when you agree with people in general but have specifics to work out; and that work can be a joy. It's anti-evangelical work you go into with an open mind, as willing to be convinced as you are eager to convince. For those inclined that way, this exploration of ideas is an adventure full of the subtle pleasures of expanding meaning and understanding, of going beyond where one started. An idea goes back and forth like a tennis ball, but one that grows and changes with every volley. It's an arrangement in which no one is the preacher or the choir, in which everything is open to question, in which ideas are beautiful and precision is holy.

Though great political work and useful debate about ideas and ethics are happening over social media, much of the time we spend together (or in solitude) has been replaced by the time we spend online, in arenas not conducive to subtlety or complexity. We have shifted to short declarative statements, to thinking in headlines, binaries, catchall categories, to viewing words as pieces in a game of checkers rather than, say, gestures in a ballet. If you're confident that everything not black is white, discussions about shades and hues seem beside the point. This absolutism presumes that our only position on those with whom we don't have complete agreement is complete disapproval, and also that agreement is simple, a finish line past which there is no nuance, strategy, possibility to explore.

Absolutism is obviously antithetical to practical politics, which, of course, depend on understanding and sometimes working alongside those with whom you may not agree, or with whom you agree on some things and not on others (as I learned in antinuclear political gatherings in the 1980s, when downwind Mormons, punks, pagans, Japanese Buddhist monks, Franciscan priests and nuns, and Western Shoshone elders worked together pretty well). Maybe it's antithetical to the human condition, where we must coexist with difference and make the most of our journeys in increments.

To dismiss the value of talking to our own is to fail to see that the value of conversation, like that of preaching, goes far beyond persuasion or the transmission of information. At its best, conversation is a means of accomplishing many subtle and indirect things.

The painter Rudolf Baranik, who died in 1998, once told me a story about a ferry ride he took in New York City on a bitter winter day in the late 1930s, soon after he had arrived as a refugee from Eastern Europe. "It is very cold, is it not?" he said in his formal English to a Black man standing next to him on the deck. "Yeaaahh, *man,*" his fellow passenger replied. "Why is that man singing?" Baranik wondered. The moment remained with him—the unfamiliar musicality of the New Yorker's intonation had made memorable an otherwise ordinary exchange, and the story remained with me. Why comment to a stranger about the weather, when the conditions are obvious to both of you? Because it's an affirmation that you exist in the same place, that no matter what else might separate you, you have this in common. And because it's an opening, if not to understanding, then at least to the place where it might begin.

Words do a lot of work that is not literal; that brief exchange about the cold created warmth between two strangers. With people one sees regularly, these little exchanges create relationships in the neighborhood, the newsstand, the hospital, the auto shop, relationships that are a pleasure and sometimes a vital resource. Prairie soil is held in place by the fine threads of root systems laid down by living and dead grasses, reaching farther below than above the surface. A sort of root system arises from these interactions, holding people together in a complex we might call a neighborhood or a community or a society, built out of feelings rather than facts.

And then there's flirting, another of life's great pleasures, in which what's exchanged might be considered information and negotiation, but of the most fizzy kind, each utterance an intoxication in itself as well as a step along the path. Which is to say that talk can be play rather than work, or it can do subtle work that is not, as Katya Lysander pointed out, about information in any practical sense.

Minister Karen Stokes told me she thinks of the choir as providing a space that is the near opposite of the combative culture of the internet. "In so many churches that I've served, the choir is the primary support group. They meet every week; they hang out together, put in extra time on Sunday, have made a commitment to one another. You can't just drop in and say, 'Let's sing this or I'm leaving.' Everyone has submitted themselves to something bigger: to the creation of music and, in the church setting, music for the worship of God."

Within most examples of broad consensus lie a host of questions and unresolved differences and possibilities. Agreement is only the foundation. Yet from here we can build strong communities of love, spirited movements of resistance. "We cannot walk alone," Dr. King said that day in 1963. In finding people to walk with—and talk with—we find power as well as pleasure.

III.
American Edges

Climate Change
Is Violence

(2014)

If you're poor, the only way you're likely to injure someone is the old, traditional way—artisanal violence, we could call it: by hands, by knife, by club; or maybe modern hands-on violence, by gun or by car.

But if you're tremendously wealthy, you can practice industrial-scale violence without any manual labor on your part. You can, say, build a sweatshop factory that will collapse in Bangladesh and kill more people than any hands-on mass murderer ever did, or you can calculate risk and benefit about putting poisons or unsafe machines into the world, as manufacturers do every day. If you're the leader of a country, you can declare war and kill by the hundreds of thousands or millions. And the nuclear superpowers—the United States and Russia—still hold the option of destroying quite a lot of life on Earth. So do the carbon barons.

But when we talk about violence, we almost always talk about violence from below, not above. Or so I thought, when I received a press release from a climate group, announcing, "Scientists say there is a direct link between changing climate and an increase in violence." What the scientists actually said, in a not so newsworthy article in *Nature*, is that there is higher conflict in the tropics in El Niño years, and that perhaps this will scale up to make our age of climate change also an era of civil and international conflict.

The message is that ordinary people will behave badly in an era of intensified climate change. All this makes sense, unless you go back to the premise and note that climate change is itself violence. Extreme, horrific, long-term, widespread violence.

Climate change is anthropogenic—caused by human beings, by some much more than by others. We know the consequences of that change: the acidification of oceans and decline of many species in them; the slow disappearance of island nations such as the Maldives; increased flooding, drought, crop failure leading to food price increases and famine; increasingly turbulent weather. (Think of the recent hurricanes in Houston, New York, Puerto Rico; the fires in California and Australia; the typhoons in the Philippines; and heat waves that kill elderly people by the tens of thousands.)

Climate change is violence.

So if we want to talk about violence and climate change, then let's talk about climate change as violence. Rather than worrying about whether ordinary human beings will react turbulently to the destruction of the very means of their survival, let's worry about that destruction—and their survival. Of course, crop failure, drought, flooding, and more will continue to lead—as they already have—to mass migration and climate refugees, and this will lead to conflict. Those conflicts are being set in motion now.

You can regard the Arab Spring, in part, as a climate conflict: the increase in wheat prices was one of the triggers for the series of revolts that changed the face of northernmost Africa and the Middle East. On the one hand, you can say, How nice if those people had not been hungry in the first place. On the other, how can you not say, How great is it that those people stood up against being deprived of sustenance and hope? And then you have to look at the systems that created that hunger—the enormous economic inequalities in places such as Egypt and the brutality used to keep down the people at the lower levels of the social system—as well as at the weather.

People revolt when their lives are unbearable. Sometimes material reality creates that unbearableness: droughts, plagues, storms, floods. But food and medical care, health and well-being, access to housing and education—these things are governed also by economic means and government policy. Climate change will increase hunger as food prices rise and food production falters, but we already have widespread hunger on Earth, and much of it is due not to the failures of nature and farmers but to systems of distribution. Almost 16 million children in the United States now live with hunger, according to the US Department of Agriculture, and that is not because the vast, agriculturally rich United States cannot produce enough to feed all of us. We are a country whose distribution system is itself a kind of violence.

Climate change is not suddenly bringing about an era of inequitable distribution. I suspect people will be revolting against in the future what they revolted against in the past: the injustices of the system. They should revolt, and we should be glad they do, if not so glad that they need to. One of the events prompting the French Revolution was the failure of the 1788 wheat crop, which made bread prices skyrocket and the poor go hungry. The insurance against such events is often thought to be more authoritarianism and more threats against the poor, but that's only an attempt to keep a lid on what's boiling over; the alternative is to turn down the heat.

The same week I received that ill-thought-out press release about climate and violence, Exxon Mobil Corporation issued a policy report. It makes for boring reading, unless you can make the dry language of business into pictures of the consequences of those acts undertaken for profit. Exxon says, "We are confident that none of our hydrocarbon reserves are now or will become 'stranded.' We believe producing these assets is essential to meeting growing energy demand worldwide."

Stranded assets means that carbon assets—coal, oil, gas still underground—would become worthless if we decided they could not be extracted and burned in the near future. Scientists advise that we need to leave most of the world's known carbon reserves in the ground if we are to go for the milder rather than the more extreme versions of climate change. Under the milder version, countless more people, living species, places will survive. In the best-case scenario, we damage the earth less. We are currently wrangling about how much to devastate the earth.

In every arena, we need to look at industrial-scale and systemic violence, not just the hands-on violence of the less powerful. When it comes to climate change, this is particularly true. Exxon has decided to bet that we can't make the corporation keep its reserves in the ground, and the company is reassuring its investors that it will continue to profit off the rapid, violent, and intentional destruction of the earth.

That's a tired phrase, destruction of the earth, but translate it into the face of a starving child and a barren field—and then multiply that a few million times. Or just picture the tiny mollusks: scallops, oysters, or Arctic sea snails that can't form shells in acidifying oceans right now. Or another superstorm tearing apart another city. Climate change is global-scale violence, against places and living species as well as against human beings. Once we call it by its true name, we can start having a real conversation about our priorities and values. Because the revolt against brutality begins with a revolt against the language that hides that brutality.

Blood on the Foundation

(2006)

The place where the teenage twins were murdered was beautiful, and the men who killed them and their uncle were to become among the most celebrated in the United States. But on that Sunday, June 28, 1846, the murder site just north of San Francisco was not in the United States. It, like the rest of California and the entire Southwest, was still Mexico, and this is why the two de Haro boys, Francisco and Ramón, were shot down in cold blood along with their elderly uncle, José de la Reyes Berreyessa.

I have imagined it as an image often enough I now see it: the three men standing up against the blue water of San Francisco Bay, wearing serapes, carrying saddles, startled, then stunned, then dead, one by one, as the gunman picked them off. There's something about those three figures against the water of the pristine bay, stark and symbolic. Blue water. Gold hills. Three upright against the beauty of the place. Then three bodies lying crumpled on the shore. It's the kind of death sung about in ballads, the kind of death that paintings are made of. No one has made much of this one, though San Rafael–born poet Robert Hass mentioned their deaths in his 1970 poem "Palo Alto: The Marshes (for Mariana Richardson 1830–1899)."

89

Some accounts put the murder scene at Point San Pedro, the semi-rustic peninsula jutting into the bay; some put it closer to Mission San Rafael, in what is now the town center. All the accounts agree that the three Mexican citizens had rowed across from Point San Pablo, north of present-day Berkeley. News in those days traveled at the speed of a horseman or a boat, and news of the seizure of Northern California's administrator, Mariano Guadalupe Vallejo, in Sonoma on June 14 may not have reached many of his fellow Californios—as the Mexican citizens of Alta, or upper, California were called. Berreyessa, however, had heard that his son José de los Santos Berreyessa, the alcade (or mayor) of Sonoma, had been taken prisoner and had rowed over with his nephews to investigate.

The little war had been brewing for a while. President James Polk had major territorial ambition, and he had sent emissary Thomas O. Larkin to encourage the Californios to defect (with their territory) to the United States. At the same time, he had pushed Great Britain to settle the dispute over the Pacific Northwest, acquiring what is now Oregon and Washington for the United States, as well as annexing the newly independent (from Mexico) Texas and starting what our school textbooks call the Mexican-American War. It might more accurately be called the War on Mexico, because we started it. When it was done, Mexico reluctantly ceded nearly half its territory—more than half a million square miles, including what is now western New Mexico and Colorado, California, Nevada, Utah, most of Arizona, and a bit of Wyoming.

Huge swaths of land—which really belonged to the Native nations that had been there long before Spain, Mexico, or Polk— transferred title in those years, and the United States assumed its modern coast-to-coast shape. But the Bear Flag Revolt wasn't epic or heroic, just a strange squabble that melded into the war against Mexico. It began when a number of Yankee settlers near Sutter

Buttes in the Central Valley, inflamed by rumors that a small army of Mexicans was coming to drive out the illegal aliens—the Americans—decided to jump the gun and seize the place. They set out in the second week of June, recruiting as they went, so that about thirty of them stole into Sonoma's plaza at dawn on June 14.

There, the illegal aliens stormed Vallejo's home and took him hostage. Some wore buckskin pants, some coyote-fur hats; some had no shoes. One account describes them as "a marauding band of horse thieves, trappers, and runaway sailors." Vallejo was a man of culture, a rancher, and a reluctant governor, not averse to being annexed by the United States but not inclined to become a prisoner or a second-class citizen. It was his open immigration policy that had created the problem in the first place. They raised a flag with a bear so badly drawn that some of the Mexicans thought it was a pig. A better version remains on the California flag, though the subspecies of grizzly on it became extinct more than eighty years ago. The ironies pile high.

Captain John Charles Frémont, who had entered California illegally with band of scouts and soldiers, egged on the revolt and then joined it, stealing horses, commandeering supplies, and pretty much doing anything he liked. The morning of June 28, he and his chief scout, Kit Carson, were near the shores of San Rafael when the de Haro twins rowed their uncle across so that he could, by some accounts, visit his son in Sonoma. Carson asked Frémont what to do about these unarmed Californios. Frémont—according to Jasper O'Farrell, who was there—waved his hand and said, "I have got no room for prisoners." So Carson, from fifty yards away, shot them. As one history relates it, "Ramón was killed as soon as he reached the shore. Francisco then threw himself down upon his brother's body. Next, a command rang out: 'Kill the other son of a bitch!' It was obeyed immediately." When the uncle asked why the boys had been killed, he was shot down, too. Berreyessa's son Antonio later ran into a Yankee wearing his father's serape—the bodies had been stripped of their clothing and left where they lay—and asked Frémont to order its return to him. Frémont refused, so Antonio Berreyessa paid the thief $25 for the garment.

. The son remained bitter for the rest of his days. The father of the twins is said to have died of grief. California became part of the United States. Carson, who had participated in a massacre of Klamath tribespeople to the north, would later murder Indians in the Mojave Desert and play a crucial role in the exile of the Navajo and the Mescalero Apache from their homelands. Later he became a popular frontier hero, the subject of many laudatory and partly fictitious books. Frémont's star rose. He became the 1856 presidential candidate for the newly founded Republican Party. He ran on an antislavery platform, but old scandals, including his commanding the murder of Berreyessa and the de Haros, surfaced. San Francisco surveyor Jasper O'Farrell testified against him in the only firsthand account of the murder, and Frémont failed to carry the state of California. Several more Berreyessa men were murdered by Yankees after the war, and the family lost its vast holdings of Bay Area land. There are far more deaths that history neglects to mention, including the deaths of those crossing the liné drawn in the sand after the Mexican-American War. It's all a reminder of the arbitrariness of borders and the color of justice.

What happened in California more than 170 years ago has everything to do with what is happening now, on the border created then and with the status of Latinos who are often treated as invaders, even when for many of them the story is, "We didn't cross the border; the border crossed us." There is another monument of a sort to all these characters. Frémont and Vallejo are streets that never quite cross in the northeast of San Francisco. Polk and Larkin run parallel to each other, farther west, crossed by O'Farrell Street. De Haro Street runs across Potrero Hill, farther south in the city, named after the father of the murdered twins, who was also the city's first mayor. Berryessa is a man-made lake that arrived on the scene much later. Carson is a pass in the Sierra Nevada, a suburb in Los Angeles, a public school in Las Vegas, and a monument in Santa Fe, while his commander, Frémont, is a city in the East Bay as well as the South Central Los Angeles high school my father graduated from. But these don't tell the story to those who don't already know the strange, bloody way California entered the United States.

Death by Gentrification

The Killing of Alex Nieto
and the Savaging
of San Francisco

(2016)

On what would have been his thirtieth birthday, Alejandro Nieto's parents left a packed courtroom in San Francisco, shortly before pictures from their son's autopsy were shown to a jury. The photographs showed what happens when fourteen bullets rip through a person's head and body. Refugio and Elvira Nieto spent much of the rest of the day sitting on a bench in the windowless hall of the federal building where their civil lawsuit for their son's wrongful death was being heard.

Alex Nieto was twenty-eight years old when he was killed in the neighborhood where he had spent his whole life. He died in a barrage of bullets fired at him by four San Francisco policemen. There are a few things about his death that everyone agrees on: he was in a hilltop park eating a burrito and tortilla chips, wearing the Taser he owned for his job as a licensed security guard at a nightclub, when someone called 911 to report him, a little after 7 pm on the evening of March 21, 2014. When police officers arrived a few minutes later, they claim Nieto defiantly pointed the Taser at them, that they mistook its red laser light for the laser sights of a gun, and they shot him in self-defense. However, the stories of the four officers contradict one other, as well as some of the evidence, and parts of their stories seem hard to believe.

On the road that curves around the green hilltop of Bernal Heights Park there is an unofficial memorial to Nieto. People walking dogs or running or taking a stroll stop to read the banner, which is pinned by stones to the slope of the hill and surrounded by fresh and artificial flowers. Alex's father, Refugio, still visits the memorial at least once a day, walking up from his small apartment on the south side of Bernal Hill. Alex Nieto had been visiting the hilltop since he was a child. That evening, March 3, 2016, his parents, joined by friends and supporters, went up there in the dark to bring a birthday cake up to the memorial.

Refugio and Elvira Nieto are dignified, modest people, straight-backed but careworn, who speak eloquently in Spanish and hardly at all in English. They had known each other as poor children in a little town in the state of Guanajuato in central Mexico and emigrated separately to the Bay Area in the 1970s, where they met again and married in 1984. They have lived in the same building on the south slope of Bernal Hill ever since. Elvira worked for decades as a housekeeper in San Francisco's downtown hotels and is now retired. Refugio had worked on the side, but mostly stayed at home as the principal caregiver of Alex and his younger brother, Hector.

In the courtroom, Hector, handsome, somber, with glossy black hair pulled back neatly, sat with his parents most days, not far from the three white and one Asian policemen who killed his brother. That there was a trial at all was a triumph. The city had withheld from family and supporters the full autopsy report and the names of the officers who shot Nieto, and it was months before the key witness overcame his fear of the police to come forward.

Nieto died because a series of white men saw him as a menacing intruder in the place he had spent his whole life. Some of them thought he was possibly a gang member because he was wearing a red jacket. Many Latino boys and men in San Francisco avoid wearing red and blue because they are the colors of two gangs, the Norteños and Sureños—but the colors of San Francisco's NFL team, the 49ers, are red and gold. Wearing a 49ers jacket in San Francisco is as ordinary as wearing a Saints jersey in New Orleans or a Yankees cap in New York. That evening, Nieto, who had thick black eyebrows and a closely cropped goatee, was wearing a new-looking 49ers jacket, a black 49ers cap, a white T-shirt, black trousers, and a belt with the holstered Taser on it, under his jacket. (Tasers shoot out wires that deliver an electrical shock, briefly paralyzing their target; they are shaped roughly like a gun, but more bulbous; Nieto's had bright yellow markings over much of its surface and a fifteen-foot range.)

Nieto was first licensed by the state as a security guard in 2007 and had worked in that field since. He had never been arrested and had no police record, an achievement in a neighborhood where Latino kids can get picked up just for hanging out in public. He was a Buddhist: a Latino son of immigrants who practiced Buddhism is the kind of hybrid San Francisco used to be good at. As a teen he had worked as a youth counselor for almost five years at the Bernal Heights Neighborhood Center; he was gregarious and community-spirited, a participant in political campaigns, street fairs, and community events.

He graduated from community college with a focus on criminal justice, and hoped to help young people as a probation officer. He had an internship with the city's juvenile probation depart-

ment not long before his death, according to former city probation officer Carlos Gonzalez, who became a friend. Gonzalez
said Nieto knew how criminal justice worked in the city. No one
has ever provided a convincing motive for why he would point a
gun-shaped object at the police when he understood that it would
probably be a fatal act.

After Nieto's death, his character was also set up for assassi-
nation. Like a rape victim, he was blamed for what had happened,
and irrelevant but unflattering things were dredged up about his
past and publicized. Immediately after his death, the police and
coroner's office dug into his medical records and found that he'd
had a crisis years before. They blew that up into a story that he was
mentally ill, to make that the explanation for what happened. It ran
like this: Why did they shoot Nieto? Because he pointed his Taser
at them and they thought it was a gun. Why did he point his Taser
at them? Because he was mentally ill. What was the evidence that
he was mentally ill? That he pointed a Taser at them. It's a circular
logic that only leads somewhere if your trust in the San Francisco
Police Department is great.

Nieto owned the Taser for his guard job at the El Toro Night
Club, whose owner, Jorge del Rio, speaks of him as a calm and
peaceful person he liked, trusted, admired, and still cares about:
"He was very calm, a very calm guy. So I was very surprised to hear
that they claim that he pulled a Taser on the police. Never have
seen him react aggressively to anyone. He was the guy who would
want to help others. I just can't believe they're saying this about
him." He told me how peaceful Nieto was, how brilliant at defus-
ing potentially volatile situations, drawing drunk men out of the
rowdy dance club with a Spanish-speaking clientele to tell them on
the street, "Tonight's not your night," and send them home feeling
liked and respected.

From the beginning the police were hoping that Alex Nieto's mental health records would somehow exonerate them. The justification that he was mentally ill got around, and it found some traction in local publications committed to exculpating the police. But it was ruled inadmissible evidence by the judge in the civil suit brought by his parents. The medical records said that Alex Nieto had some sort of breakdown and was treated for it three years earlier. Various terms were thrown around—psychosis, paranoid schizophrenia—but the entire file was from 2011, and there seemed to be no major preceding or subsequent episodes of note. The theory that mental illness is relevant presumes not only that he was mentally ill on March 21, 2014, but that mental illness caused him to point a Taser at the police. If you don't believe he pointed a Taser at the police, then mental illness doesn't supply any clues to what happened. Did he? The only outside witness to the shooting says he did not.

Here's the backstory as I heard it from a family friend: devastated by a breakup, Alex got very dramatic about it one day, burned some love letters, and was otherwise acting out in the tiny apartment the four Nietos shared. His exasperated family called a city hotline for help in deescalating the situation, but got the opposite: Nieto was seized and institutionalized against his will. The records turned burning the love letters into burning a book or trying to burn down the house—something may have been lost in translation from Spanish.

That was in early 2011; there was another incident later that year. In 2012, 2013, and until his death in 2014, he appears to have been a calm, reasonable, well-functioning young man with exceptional altruism and generosity in his dealings with others. There is no reason to believe that, even if what transpired in 2011 should be classified as mental illness, he suddenly relapsed on the evening of his death, after years of being tranquil in the chaos of his nightclub job. And shortly before his encounter with the police, he exercised restraint in a confrontation with an aggressor.

◆

On the evening of March 21, 2014, Evan Snow, a thirtysomething "user experience design professional," according to his LinkedIn profile, who had moved to the neighborhood about six months earlier (and who has since departed for a more suburban location), took his young Siberian husky for a walk on Bernal Hill. As Snow was leaving the park, Nieto was coming up one of the little dirt trails that leads to the park's ring road, eating chips. In a deposition prior to the trial, Snow said that with his knowledge of the attire of gang members, he "put Nieto in that category of people that I would not mess around with."

His dog put Nieto in the category of people carrying food, and went after him. In his three accounts of the subsequent events, Snow never seemed to recognize that his out-of-control dog was the aggressor: "So Luna was, I think, looking to move around the benches or behind me to run up happily to get a chip from Mr. Nieto. Mr. Nieto became further—what's the right word?—distressed, moving very quickly and rapidly left to right, trying to keep his chips away from Luna. He ran down to these benches and jumped up on the benches, my dog following. She was at that point vocalizing, barking, or kind of howling." The dog had Nieto cornered on the bench while its inattentive owner was forty feet away—in his deposition for the case, under oath, his exact words were that he was distracted by a woman "jogger's butt." Snow said, "I can imagine that somebody would—could assume the dog was being aggressive at that point." The dog did not come when he called, but kept barking.

Nieto, according to Snow, then pulled back his jacket and took his Taser out, briefly pointing it at the distant dog owner before he pointed the weapon at the dog baying at his feet. The two men yelled at each other, and Snow apparently used a racial slur, but would not later give the precise word. As he left the park, he texted a friend about the incident. His text, according to his testimony, said, "In another state like Florida, I would have been justified in shooting Mr. Nieto that night"—a reference to that state's infamous Stand Your Ground law, which removes the obligation to retreat before using force in self-defense. In other words, he apparently wished he could have done what George Zimmerman did to Trayvon Martin in 2012: execute him without consequences.

Soon after, a couple out walking their dogs passed by Nieto. Tim Isgitt, then a recent arrival to the area, is the communications director of a nonprofit organization founded by tech billionaires. He now lives in suburban Marin County, as does his husband, Justin Fritz, a self-described "email marketing manager," who had lived in San Francisco about a year. In a picture one of them posted on social media, they are chestnut-haired, clean-cut white men posing with their dogs, a springer spaniel and an old bulldog. They were walking those dogs when they passed Nieto at a distance.

Fritz did not notice anything unusual, but Isgitt saw Nieto moving "nervously" and putting his hand on the Taser in its holster. Snow was gone, so Isgitt had no idea that Nieto had just had an ugly altercation and had reason to be disturbed. Isgitt began telling people he encountered to avoid the area. (One witness who did see Nieto shortly after Isgitt and Fritz, longtime Bernal Heights resident Robin Bullard, who was walking his own dog in the park, testified that there was nothing alarming about Nieto. "He was just sitting there," Bullard said.)

At the trial, Fritz testified that he had not seen anything alarming about Nieto. He said that he called 911 because Isgitt urged him to. At about 7:11 pm he began talking to the 911 dispatcher, telling her that there was a man with a black handgun. What race, asked the dispatcher, "Black, Hispanic?" "Hispanic," replied Fritz. Later, the dispatcher asked him if the man in question was doing "anything violent," and Fritz answered, "Just pacing, it looks like he might be eating chips or sunflowers, but he's resting a hand kind of on the gun." Alex Nieto had about five more minutes to live.

◆

San Francisco, like all cities, has been a place where, when newcomers arrive in a trickle, they integrate and contribute to the ongoing transformation of a place that has never been static in demographics and industries. When they arrive in a flood, as they have during economic booms since the nineteenth-century gold rush, including the dot-com surge of the late 1990s and the current tech tsunami, they scour out what was there before. By 2012, the incursion of tech workers had gone from steady stream to deluge, and more and more people and institutions—bookstores, churches, social services, nonprofits of all kinds, gay and lesbian bars, small businesses with deep roots in the neighborhoods—began to be evicted. So did seniors, including many in their nineties, schoolteachers, working-class families, the disabled, and pretty much anyone who was a tenant whose home could be milked for more money.

San Francisco had been a place where some people came out of idealism, or stayed to realize an ideal: to work for social justice or teach the disabled, to write poetry or practice alternative medicine—to be part of something larger than themselves that was not a corporation, to live for something more than money. That has become less and less possible as rent and home prices spiral upward. What the old-timers were afraid of losing, many of the newcomers seemed unable to recognize. The tech culture seemed in small and large ways to be a culture of disconnection and withdrawal.

And it was very white, male, and young. In 2014, Google's Silicon Valley employees, for example, were 2 percent Black, 3 percent Latino, and 70 percent male. The Google Bus—private luxury shuttles—made it convenient for these employees who worked on the peninsula to live in San Francisco, as did shuttles for Facebook, Apple, Yahoo, and other big corporations. Airbnb, headquartered in San Francisco, became the means of transforming long-term housing stock in rural and urban places around the world into space for upscale transients. Uber, also based here, set about undermining taxi companies that paid a living wage. Another tech company housed here, Twitter, is notorious for letting hate speech and death threats against vulnerable and minority voices go unchecked. San Francisco, once a utopia in the eyes of many, became the nerve center of a new dystopia.

Tech companies created multimillionaires and billionaires whose influence warped local politics, pushing for policies that served the new industry and their employees at the expense of the rest of the population. None of the money sloshing around the city trickled down to preserve the center for homeless youth that closed in 2013; or the oldest Black-owned, Black-focused bookstore in the country, which closed in 2014; or San Francisco's last lesbian bar, which folded in 2015; or the Latino drag and trans bar that closed the year before. As the Nieto trial unfolded, the uniquely San Franciscan Saint John Coltrane African Orthodox Church faced eviction from the home it had found after an earlier eviction during the late-1990s dot-com boom. That spring, the Sierra Club—perhaps the greatest flagship of San Francisco idealism and altruism, born in the city's downtown in 1892—left in pursuit of affordable rent. Other nonprofits, social services, cultural and spiritual centers were squeezed out. Resentments rose. And cultures clashed.

At 7:12 pm on the evening of March 21, 2014, the police dispatcher who had spoken to Fritz put out a call. Some police officers began establishing a periphery, a standard way to deescalate a potentially dangerous situation. One police car broke through the periphery to create a confrontation. In it were lieutenant Jason Sawyer and officer Richard Schiff, a rookie who had been on the job for less than three months. They headed for Bernal Heights Park when they got the call, tried first to enter it in their patrol car from the south side, the side where Alex's parents lived, then turned around and drove in from the north side, going around the barrier that keeps vehicles out, and heading up the road that is often full of runners, walkers, and dogs at that time of the evening. They moved rapidly and without lights or sirens. They were not heading into an emergency, but they were rushing past their fellow officers and the periphery without coordinating a plan.

At 7:17:40 pm, Alejandro Nieto came walking downhill around a bend in the road, according to the 911 operator's conversation with Fritz. At 7:18:08 pm, another policeman in the park, but not at the scene, broadcast: "Got a guy in a red shirt coming toward you." Officer Schiff testified in court, "Red could be related to a gang involvement. Red is a Norteño color." Schiff testified that from about ninety feet away he shouted, "Show me your hands," and that Nieto had replied, "No, show me your hands," then drew his Taser, assuming a fighting stance, holding the weapon in both hands, pointed at the police. The officers claim that the Taser projected a red light, which they assumed was the laser sight of a handgun, and feared for their lives. At 7:18:43 pm, Schiff and Sawyer began barraging Nieto with .40-caliber bullets.

At 7:18:55 pm, Schiff shouted "red," a police code word for out of ammunition. He had emptied a whole clip at Nieto. He reloaded and began shooting again, firing twenty-three bullets in all.

Lieutenant Sawyer was also blazing away. He fired twenty bullets. Their aim appears to have been sloppy, because Fritz, who had taken refuge in a grove of eucalyptus trees below the road, can be heard shouting, "Help! Help!" on his call to the 911 operator, as bullets fired by the police were "hitting the trees above me, breaking things and just coming at me."

Sawyer said: "Once I realized there was no reaction, none at all after being shot, I picked up my sights and aimed for the head." Nieto was hit just above the lip by a bullet that shattered his right upper jaw and teeth. Another ripped through both bones of his lower right leg while he was standing. Though the officers testify that he remained facing them, that latter bullet went in the side of his leg, as though he had turned away. That while so agonizingly injured he remained focused on pretending to menace the police with a useless device that drew fire to him is hard to believe.

Two more officers, Roger Morse and Nate Chew, drove up to the first patrol car, got out, and drew their guns. There was no plan, no communication, no strategy to contain the person they were pursuing or capture him alive if he proved to be a menace, no attempt to avoid a potentially dangerous confrontation in a popular park where bystanders could be hit. Morse testified in court that Nieto was still upright: "When I first arrived I saw what appeared to be muzzle flash. I aimed at him and began shooting." Tasers produce nothing that resembles muzzle flash. Chew, in contrast to his partner's account, testified that Nieto was already on the ground when they arrived. He fired five shots at the man on the ground. He told the court he stopped when "I saw the suspect's head fall down to the pavement."

Several more bullets hit Nieto while he was on the ground—a total of at least fourteen hit him overall, according to the city autopsy report. Only a quarter of the bullets the officers fired reached their target—they fired fifty-nine in all into the popular public park at dusk that first day of spring. They were shooting to kill, and to over-kill. One went into Alex Nieto's left temple and tore through his head toward his neck. Several hit him in the back, chest, and shoulders. One more went into the small of his back, severing his spinal cord.

The officers approached Nieto at 7:19:20 pm, less than two min-utes after it had all begun. Morse was the first to get there; he says that Nieto's eyes were open and that he was gasping and gurgling. He says that he kicked the Taser out of the dying man's hands. Schiff says he "handcuffed him, rolled him over, and said, 'Sarge, he's got a pulse.'" By the time the ambulance arrived, Alejandro Nieto was dead.

Nieto's funeral, on April 1, 2014, packed the little church in Bernal Heights that his mother had taken him to as a child. I went with my friend Adriana Camarena, a civic-minded lawyer from Mexico City who lives in the Mission District, the neigh-borhood on Bernal's north flank that has been a capital of Latino culture since the 1960s. She had met Alex briefly; I never had. We sat near a trio of African American women who lost their own sons in police killings and routinely attend the funerals of other such victims. Afterward, Adriana became close to Refugio and Elvira Nieto. Their son had been their ambassador to the English-speaking world, and gradually Adriana was drawn into their grief and their need. She stepped in as an interpreter, advocate, counsel, and friend. Benjamin Bac Sierra, a novelist and former marine who teaches writing at San Francisco's community college, had been a devoted friend of and mentor to Alex. Both organized the commu-nity in response to Nieto's killing.

In that springtime of Nieto's death, I had begun to believe that what was tearing my city apart was not only a conflict pitting long-term tenants against affluent newcomers and the landlords, real-estate agents, house-flippers, and developers seeking to open up room for themselves by shoving everyone else out. It was a conflict between two different visions of the city.

What I felt strongly at the funeral was the vital force of real community: people who experienced where they lived as a fabric woven from memory, ritual and habit, affection and love. This was a measure of place that had nothing to do with money and owner-ship—and everything to do with connection. Adriana and I turned around in our pew and met Oscar Salinas, a big man born and raised in the Mission. He told us that when someone in the community is hurt, the Mission comes together. "We take care of each other." To him, the Mission meant the people who shared Latino identity and a commitment to a set of values, and to each other, all held together by place. It was a beautiful vision that many shared.

The sense of community people were trying to hang on to was about the things that money cannot buy. It was about home as a whole neighborhood and the neighbors in it, not just the real es-tate you held title to or paid rent on. It was not only the treasure of Latinos; white, Black, Asian, and Native American residents of San Francisco had long-term relationships with people, insti-tutions, traditions, particular locations. "Disruption" has been a favorite word of the new tech economy, but old-timers saw homes, communities, traditions, and relationships being disrupted. Many of the people being evicted and priced out were the people who held us all together: teachers, nurses, counselors, social workers, carpen-ters and mechanics, volunteers and activists. When, for example, someone who worked with gang kids was driven out, those kids were abandoned. How many threads could you pull out before the social fabric disintegrated?

Two months before the funeral, the real estate website Redfin concluded that 83 percent of California's homes, and 100 percent of

San Francisco's, were unaffordable on a teacher's salary. One of the most high-profile eviction cases involved a Google lawyer trying to evict Mission District schoolteachers to merge their longtime homes into a mansion for himself. What happens to a place when the most vital workers cannot afford to live in it? Displacement has contributed to deaths, particularly of the elderly. In the years since Nieto's death, many seniors have died during or immediately after their evictions. Several were in their nineties; more than one turned a hundred while fighting eviction from her long-term home. Seventy-one percent of the homeless in San Francisco used to be housed here, a recent survey reported. Losing their homes makes them vulnerable to a host of conditions, some of them deadly. Gentrification can be fatal.

It also brings white newcomers to neighborhoods with non-white populations, sometimes with appalling consequences. *The East Bay Express* reported that in Oakland, recently arrived white people sometimes regard "people of color who are walking, driving, hanging out, or living in the neighborhood" as "criminal suspects." Some use the website Nextdoor.com to post comments "labeling Black people as suspects simply for walking down the street, driving a car, or knocking on a door." The same thing happens in the Mission, where people post things on Nextdoor, such as "I called the police a few times when is more then [*sic*] three kids standing like soldiers in the corner"; chat with each other about homeless people as dangers who need to be removed; justify police killings others see as criminal. What's clear in the case of Nieto's death is that a series of white men perceived him as more dangerous than he was, and that he died of it.

On March 1, 2016, the day the trial began, hundreds of students at San Francisco public schools walked out of class to protest Nieto's killing. A big demonstration was held in front of the federal courthouse, with drummers, Aztec dancers in feathered regalia, people holding signs, and a TV station interviewing Bac Sierra, dressed in the first of the several suits and ties he'd wear to the trial. Nieto's face on posters, banners, T-shirts, and murals had become a familiar sight in the Mission; a few videos about the case had been made, demonstrations and memorials had been held. For some, Nieto stood for victims of police brutality and for a Latino community that felt imperiled by gentrification, by the wave of evictions and the people who regarded them as menaces and intruders in their own neighborhood. Many people who cared about the Nietos came to the trial each day, and the courtroom was usually nearly full.

Trials are theater, and this one had its dramas. Adante Pointer, a Black lawyer with the Oakland firm of John L. Burris, which handles a lot of local police-killing lawsuits, represented Refugio and Elvira Nieto, the plaintiffs. Their star witness, Antonio Theodore, had come forward months after the killing. Theodore is an immigrant from Trinidad, a musician in the band Afrolicious, and a resident of the Bernal area. An elegant man with neat shoulder-length dreads who came to court in a suit, he said he had been on a trail above the road, walking a dog, and that he had seen the whole series of events unfold. He testified that Nieto's hands were in his pockets; he had not pointed his Taser at the officers; there was no red laser light; the officers had just shouted "stop" and then opened fire.

When Pointer asked him why he had not come forward earlier, he replied, "Just think: it would be hard to tell an officer that I just saw fellow officers shooting up somebody. I didn't trust the police." Theodore testified cogently under questioning from Pointer. But the next morning, when deputy city attorney Margaret Baumgartner, an imposing white woman with a resentful air, questioned him, he fell apart. He contradicted his earlier testimony about where he had been and where the shooting took place, then declared that he was an alcoholic with memory problems. He seemed to be trying to make himself safe by making himself useless. Pointer questioned him again, and he said: "I don't care to be here right now. I feel threatened." When witnesses are mistrustful or fearful of police, justice is hard to come by, and Theodore seemed terrified of them.

The details of what had happened were hotly debated and often contradictory, especially with regard to the Taser. The police had testified as though Nieto had been a superhuman or inhuman opponent, facing them off even as they fired into his body again and again, then dropping to a "tactical sniper posture" on the ground, still holding the Taser with its red laser pointing at them. The city lawyers brought in a Taser expert whose official testimony seemed to favor them, but when he was asked by Pointer to look at the crime scene photos, he said the Taser was off and that it was not something easily or accidentally turned on or off. Was Nieto busy toggling the small on/off switch while also being hammered by the bullets that killed him on the spot? The light is only on when the Taser is on. Officer Morse testified that when he arrived to kick the Taser out of Nieto's hands there was no red light or wires coming from it. The Taser wires are, however, visible in the police photographs documenting the scene.

The Taser expert told the court that the Taser's internal record said the trigger had been pulled three times. The Taser's internal clock documented these trigger pulls on March 22, after Nieto was dead. The expert witness testified that the clock was set to Greenwich Mean Time, and that he had recalculated the time to place these trigger pulls at 7:14 pm the night Nieto died. The police didn't have contact with him until 7:18 pm. The Taser expert then created a new theory of "clock drift," under which Nieto's Taser fired at exactly the right time to corroborate the police version that the Taser was on and used at the time they shot him. Even if the trigger was pulled, that's not evidence he was pointing the Taser at them. When a Taser is fired, confetti-like marker tags are ejected; none were found at the scene of the crime. Taser has since negotiated a two-million-dollar contract with the San Francisco Police Department.

One piece of evidence produced was a fragment of bone found in the pocket of Nieto's jacket. Some thought this proved that his hands had been in his pockets, as Theodore said. Dr. Amy Hart, the scandal-ridden city coroner, said in the trial on Friday, March 4, that there were no photographs of his red 49ers jacket, which must have been full of bullet holes. The following Monday, an expert witness for the city mentioned the photographs of the jacket that the city had supplied him. The jurors were shown photographs of Nieto's hat, which had a bullet hole in it that corresponded to the hole in his temple, and of his broken sunglasses lying next to a puddle of blood. The coroner testified to abrasions on Nieto's face consistent with his wearing glasses.

Before this evidence was shown, officer Richard Schiff had testified under oath that he made eye contact with Nieto and saw his forehead pucker up in a frown. If the dead man had been wearing a cap and dark glasses, then Schiff could not have seen these things. Finally, how could four police officers fire fifty-nine bullets at someone without noticing that he was not firing back? And what does it mean that they reported "muzzle flash" from an object incapable of producing it?

When Elvira Nieto testified about her devastation at the death of her son, Pointer asked her about her husband's feelings as well. "Objection," shouted Baumgartner, as though what a wife said about her husband's grief should be disqualified as hearsay. The judge overruled her. At another point, Justin Fritz apologized to the Nietos for the outcome of his 911 call, and appeared distressed. Refugio Nieto allowed Fritz to hug him; his wife did not. "Refugio later said that at that moment he was reminded of Alex's words," Adriana told me, "that even with the people that we have conflict with, we need to take the higher ground and show the best of ourselves."

Adriana sat with the Nietos every day of the trial, translating for them when the court-appointed translator was off duty. Bac Sierra, in an impeccable suit and tie, was right behind them every day, in the first of three rows of benches usually full of friends and supporters. Nieto's uncle often attended, as did Ely Flores, a young Latino who was Nieto's best friend and a fellow Buddhist, who had joined a Buddhist group when he was only eleven. Flores later told me that he and Alex had tried to support each other in living up to their vows and ideals. He said that they wanted to be "pure lotuses" in their communities, a reference to the Buddhist idea of being "a pure lotus in muddy water," something spiritual that arises but doesn't separate from the messiness of everyday life.

Flores had been studying to be a police officer at City College, seeing this as the way he could be of service to his community, but when Nieto was killed, he told me, he realized he could never wear a badge or carry a gun. He abandoned the career he'd worked toward for years and started over, training in a culinary academy as a chef. He suggested that Nieto didn't see the police as adversaries and thought that he might instead not have understood that they were coming for him when he walked around the bend in the road that evening. He had perhaps not acted according to the unwritten rules for men of color, who are considered suspects and menaces in everyday life and have to constantly signal their noncriminality through restrictions on dress, movement, and location.

Another Latino friend of Nieto's told journalist Sana Saleem that he had warned Nieto that wearing his Taser might endanger him, but said he shrugged off the cautions. You could argue that Alex Nieto died of his confidence in the right to be himself in the park he'd gone to all his life, wearing what he wanted, being who he was without reference to white fear. It had worked in the old Bernal Heights, a diverse neighborhood of people used to coexisting with difference; it did not work when the place changed.

It was a civil trial, so the standard was not "beyond a reasonable doubt," just a "preponderance of evidence." No one was facing prison, but if the city and officers were found liable, there could be a large financial settlement and it could affect the careers of the policemen. The trial was covered by many journalists from local TV stations and newspapers. On Thursday, March 10, 2016, after an afternoon and morning of deliberations, the eight jurors—five white, one Asian woman and two Asian men, none Black, none Latino—unanimously ruled in favor of the police on all counts. Flores wept in the hallway. The American Civil Liberties Union of Northern California published a response to the verdict headlined, "Would Alex Nieto Still Be Alive If He Were White?" Police are now investigating claims that Officer Morse posted a sneering attack on Nieto on a friend's Facebook page the night of the verdict.

San Francisco is now a cruel place and a divided one. A month before the trial, the city's mayor decided to sweep the homeless off the streets for the Super Bowl, even though the game was played forty miles away, at the new 49ers stadium in Silicon Valley. Online rants about the city's homeless population have become symptomatic of the city's culture clash. An open letter to the mayor posted on the Internet in February 2016 by Justin Keller, founder of a not very successful startup, was typical in its tone:

> I know people are frustrated about gentrification happening in the city, but the reality is, we live in a free market society. The wealthy working people have earned their right to live in the city. They went out, got an education, work hard, and earned it. I shouldn't have to worry about being accosted. I shouldn't

have to see the pain, struggle, and despair of homeless people
to and from my way to work every day.

And like Evan Snow, who wanted to blow away Alejandro Nieto after their encounter, Keller got his wish in a way. Pushed out of other
areas, hundreds of homeless people began to set up tents under the
freeway overpass around Division Street on the edge of the Mission,
a gritty industrial area with few residences. The mayor destroyed
this rainy-season refuge, too: city workers threw tents and belongings into dump trucks and hounded the newly propertyless onward.
An advocate for the homeless photographed the walker relied upon
by a disabled man as it was crushed by a garbage truck. One of the
purges came before dawn the morning the Nieto trial began.

When the trial ended with a verdict in favor of the police, 150 or
so people gathered inside at the Mission Cultural Center for Latino
Arts and outside on rainy Mission Street. People were composed,
resolute, disappointed, but far from shocked. It was clear that most
of them had never counted on the legal system to validate that what
happened to Alex Nieto was wrong. Their sense of principle and
history was not going to be swayed by this verdict, even if they were
saddened or angered by it. Bac Sierra, out of his courtroom suits
and in a T-shirt and cap, spoke passionately, as did Oscar Salinas,
who had just posted on Facebook the words: "Alex you will never
be forgotten, your parents will always be taken care of by us, the
community. As I've always said, the unspoken word of La Misión is
when someone is hurting, needs help, or passes we come together as
a family and take care of them." The two burly men knelt to steady
the chair on which a young woman stood up to speak.

The Nietos spoke, with Adriana translating for those who did
not understand Spanish. And Adriana spoke on her own behalf:
"One of the most important changes in my path being involved in
the Alex Nieto case has been to learn more about restorative practic-

es, because as someone trained in legal systems, I know that the pain and fear that we are not safe from police in our communities will not go away until there is personal accountability by those who harm us."

Adriana, her historian husband, and their friends, including a longtime AIDS activist and a queer choreographer, who all live nearby in a ramshackle old building, had faced their own recent eviction battle, and won. But the community that came together that night was still vulnerable to the economic forces tearing the city apart. Many of these people may have to move on soon; some already have.

The death of Alex Nieto is a story of one young man torn apart by bullets, and of a community coming together to remember him. They pursued more than justice, as the case became a cause, as the expressions became an artistic outpouring in videos, posters, and memorials, and as friendships and alliances were forged and strengthened. In 2015, a year after Nieto's killing, twenty-one-year-old indigenous immigrant Amilcar Perez-Lopez was shot to death by police who claimed they were defending themselves from a knife attack, though he died of four bullets to his back and one to the side of his head. On April 7, 2016, less than a month after the Nieto trial, the police shot longtime San Franciscan Luis Góngora to death, claiming he was rushing them with a knife. Eyewitnesses from the little homeless community he was part of and from surrounding buildings, as well as a security video, suggested otherwise. People became angrier about the police they saw as part of a city government and economic tsunami together wiping out the Black and Latino communities.

In late April 2016, five people—a grandmother and four young men of color—went on a hunger strike in front of the Mission police station, fasting for eighteen days in their Hunger for Justice campaign to force the police chief to resign. Conventional wisdom dismissed their perspective and their effort. A few weeks later, on the day that police killed Jessica Nelson Williams, an unarmed, Black, pregnant mother in her twenties, police chief Greg Suhr was forced to resign. At a demonstration that night, at the industrial site where Williams died of a single bullet, two women held a banner that said, "We are the last 3%." The Black population of San Francisco has plummeted since its peak in the 1970s, when one in six inhabitants was Black. Down the block, tucked under a freeway overpass, gentrifying homes were visible, styled in what you could call fortress modernism. The same day that Suhr resigned and Williams was killed just south of the Mission, a dozen Nextdoor users took to the site's Mission District forum to praise and express their gratitude to Suhr, who, as chief of police, had justified the San Francisco police shootings, often by lying about the facts in the cases.

At the gathering after the verdict, on the spring equinox that was also the anniversary of Alex Nieto's killing, Adriana Camarena told the crowd: "Our victory, as the Nietos said yesterday, is that we are still together."

But many forces threaten that togetherness.

No Way In, No Way Out

(2016)

Chances are that you are living the good life, at least in the most fundamental sense. You have the liberty to leave your home and the security of a home you can return to; privacy and protection, on the one hand, and work, pleasure, social encounter, exploration, and engagement, on the other. This is almost a definition of quality of life, the balance of public and private, the confidence that you have a place in the world—or a place and the world.

In the years since the Reagan Revolution, this basic condition of well-being has become unavailable to millions in the United States: the unhoused and the imprisoned. The former live in an outside without access to the inside that is shelter, home, and stability; the latter live in an inside without access to the outside that is liberty. Both suffer a chronic lack of privacy and agency.

Their ranks are vast, including 2.2 million prisoners and, at any given time, between half a million and 1.5 million people without homes. These people are regarded as disposable; prison and the streets are where they've been disposed. Prison and the streets: the two are closely related, and they feed each other in the general manner of vicious circles. Prisoners exit with few resources to integrate themselves back into the world of work and housing, which sometimes leads them straight onto the street. People living on the street are often criminalized for their everyday activities, which can put them in prison.

In San Francisco, local laws ban sitting or lying down on sidewalks and sleeping in public parks, as well as public urination and defecation—doing the things you do inside your house, the things biology requires that we all do. Many people who lack homes of their own are invisible, living in vehicles, staying overnight in workplaces, riding the night bus, couch surfing, and looking like everyone else. The most devastated and marginalized are the most visible. Even they try to keep a low profile: I walk past the unhoused daily, seeing how they seek to disappear, situating their camps behind big-box stores and alongside industrial sites, where they are less likely to inspire the housed to call for their removal.

The young can't remember (and many of their elders hardly recall) that few people were homeless before the 1980s. They don't grasp that this problem doesn't have to exist, that we could largely end it, as we could many other social problems, with little more radical a solution than a return to the buffered capitalism of forty years ago, when real wages were higher, responsibility for taxes more equitably distributed, and a far stronger safety net caught more of those who fell. Homelessness has been created by federal, state, and local policies—not just by defunding mental-health programs, which is too often cited as the cause. Perfectly sane people lose access to housing every day, though the resulting ordeal may undermine some of that sanity, as it might yours and mine.

In our antitax era, many cities fish for revenue by taxing the homeless, turning the police into de facto bill collectors. Those unable to pay the fines and warrants for panhandling, loitering, or sleeping outdoors—meaning most people forced to panhandle, loiter, or sleep outdoors in the first place—can be hauled into court at any time. As

Astra Taylor observes, "Municipal budgets are overly reliant on petty infraction penalties because affluent, mostly white citizens have been engaged in a 'tax revolt' for decades, lobbying for lower rates and special treatment." Black Lives Matter has in part been a rebellion against this criminalization of poverty and in particular the police persecution of African Americans for minor infractions.

The situation is particularly bitter in San Francisco, now annexed as part of Silicon Valley, since the tech industry created a gigantic bubble of wealth that puts economic inequality in much sharper relief. Here is Mark Zuckerberg, the fifth-richest person in the world, in his house on the western edge of the historically Latino and working-class Mission District. Here is Division Street, on the northern edge of that neighborhood, where more than 250 housing-deprived people settled in tents early in 2016, seeking shelter from both the rain and the mayor's sweeps of the homeless as he primped the city for Super Bowl visitors.

Of course, being homeless is itself hard work—over the thirty-six years that I've observed the indigent in San Francisco, they have often made me think of hunter-gatherers. These people forage for survival, eluding attack, roaming, watching, maybe making the rounds of social services and soup kitchens, trying to protect what possessions they have, starting over from nothing when medications, phones, and documents are stolen by compatriots or seized by police. The city is a wilderness to them; that they now live in tents designed for recreational camping makes it all the more ironic. Photographer Robert Gumpert notes that some feel they cannot leave their tents for even short lengths of time, for fear of losing their belongings. Others suffer from sleep deprivation, since they can find no safe place to rest.

Those without houses are too often regarded as problems to people rather than as people with problems. No wonder the means of addressing them is often that used to address litter, dirt, and contamination: removal. "If you're trying to prevent the undesirables from using park bathrooms, adding porta potties seems like a pretty decent solution," commented a Mission resident named Branden on an online neighborhood forum. "If you're trying to keep the dirty undesirables away forever, you'll need constant police presence with a mandate to use violence to enforce whatever law prohibits their existence."

Bird in a Cage:

Visiting Jarvis Masters on Death Row

(2016)

There are two things I think about nearly every time I row out into San Francisco Bay. One is a passage from Shankar Vedantam's *The Hidden Brain*, in which he talks about a swim he once took. A decent swimmer in his own estimate, Vedantam went out into the sea one day and felt that he had become superb and powerful; he was instantly proud of his new abilities. Far from shore, he realized he had been riding a current and was going to have to fight it all the way back to shore. "Unconscious bias influences our lives in exactly the same manner as that undercurrent," Vedantam writes. "Those who travel with the current will always feel they are good swimmers; those who swim against the current may never realize they are better swimmers than they imagine."

Most mornings I row out against the current, and the moment when I turn around is exhilarating. Strokes that felt choppy and ineffectual are suddenly graceful and powerful. I feel very good at what I do, even though I know that the tide is going my way.

Rowing is the closest I will ever come to flying. On calm, flat days my battered old oars make twin circles of ripples that spread out until they intersect behind the stern of the boat. I'm forever retreating from that gentle disturbance, the water smoothing itself into glass again as I go. On the calmest days, when the bay is a mirror, these oars pull me and my scull through reflected clouds in long glides, the two nine-foot oars moving together like wings in that untrammeled space.

The birds are one of the great joys, the terns and pelicans and gulls, the coots and stilts and cormorants, who dive and fly and float, living in the air and the water and the plane between them. The freedom of rowing is enlarged by the freedom of the birds. I set out from the estuary of Corte Madera Creek as it pours into San Francisco Bay. En route I pass Point San Quentin, and San Quentin Prison.

When I row past the prison I think about currents and I think about Jarvis Jay Masters, who's been on my mind for a long time. We were born eight months apart, to the day, and are both children of coastal California. We're both storytellers. But he has been in San Quentin since he was nineteen, more than a third of a century, and has swum against the current all his life. For the past twenty-five years, he's been on death row, though the evidence is on the side of his innocence.

Until he turned twenty-three, Masters's story could have been that of any number of poor inner-city boys: his father, missing in action; his mother, drawn into the vortex of heroin; his early neglect; and a ride through the best and then the worst of the foster care system, which dropped him straight into the juvenile prison system. At nineteen, he was sent to San Quentin for armed robbery. Four years later, on June 8, 1985, Howell Burchfield, a San Quentin prison guard and father of five, was murdered. Two members of a Black prison gang were convicted of planning and carrying out the crime. They were given life sentences. Masters was accused of conspiring in the murder and sharpening the weapon used to stab Burchfield in the heart. He received the death penalty.

In books and movies, resourceful lawyers or investigators find a subtle detail, possibly two, to undermine an otherwise credible case. But in Masters's case there aren't merely one or two weak links. So far as I can tell, the whole chain is rotten. Major witnesses changed their testimony, and several of the prisoners who testified against Masters recanted. Some testified that they had been offered incentives to incriminate him. One star witness was so unreliable and so widely used as an informant that dozens of cases in the state had to be thrown out because of his involvement. He has recanted his testimony about Masters. The man convicted of the stabbing said in 2004 that Masters was innocent and that all three men on trial were "under orders from [gang] commanders that, under threat of death, none of us could discuss the [gang] in any way." In other words, Masters faced two death penalties, and one set him up for the other.

I first read about Masters in *Altars in the Street*, a 1997 book by Melody Ermachild Chavis, the defense investigator for his murder trial. They have remained close for thirty years. Chavis and I later became friends. "It was obvious ... even way back then, between 1985 and 1990, that they had a lot of suspects and a lot of theories," she told me. "The big mistake they made was: they destroyed the crime scene. They bagged it all up and threw it in the Marin County dump."

She described the way prisoners and prison officials got rid of hundreds of notes that had been exchanged between prisoners, as well as a large collection of prison-made knives, which had been thrown out of the cells when the prisoners realized that they were going to be searched. According to one account in Masters's mountain of legal documents, guards collected two different potential murder weapons, which they said they put into envelopes as evidence. Both disappeared before the trial.

Masters was a gang member at the time of the killing, but the gang's leaders eventually gave many reasons why it was impossible that he had sharpened the missing weapon. One was that he had voted against killing Burchfield, an act of insubordination for which he had been stripped of responsibilities. Another was geography; he was on the fourth tier of a cell block, and the murder took place on the second tier. Moving a weapon back and forth would have been difficult and dangerous, and a witness testified that the weapon never left the second tier. Too, someone else admitted to making it.

Masters's attorneys filed the opening brief of his appeal in 2001, after which his case progressed slowly. It was not until November 2015 that the California Supreme Court heard oral arguments on the appeal. Even by the standards of California's glacial appeals process, this is an unusually long time.

Though only 6.5 percent of Californians are Black, African Americans make up 29 percent of the state's incarcerated and 36 percent of those condemned to death. They are more likely than others convicted of similar crimes to receive the death penalty, and assailants of any race convicted of killing a white person are far more likely to be sentenced to death than if the victim is of another race. There are those who swim with the current and those who swim against it, and then there are those who have fire hoses turned on them.

The first time I saw Masters was at a session of a 2011 evidentiary hearing. There, in the small courtroom, stood a tall, gracious man in shackles and an orange jumpsuit. A dozen or so friends and supporters were present, most of them from the Buddhist community. Since his sentencing, Masters had become a devoted Buddhist practitioner. He told me that he meditates daily and tries to incorporate teachings about compassion into his daily life among prisoners and guards. In 1989, he took vows from Chagdud Tulku Rinpoche, an exiled Tibetan lama and distinguished teacher who died in 2002. (The first vow was "From this day forward I will not hurt or harm other people even if it costs my life.") Masters has since prevented violence and suicide, comforted the devastated, and encouraged the growth of fellow prisoners, and despite the crime he's accused of is clearly liked and trusted by the guards. Pema Chödrön, a writer and abbess who is perhaps the best-known Buddhist in the West after the Dalai Lama, speaks of Masters with admiration, and visits him every year.

When we began talking on the phone, in late 2015, Masters told me how much prisoners crave connection with the outside world. Buddhism allowed him to join a community of ethical and idealistic people with practical ideas about how to respond to suffering and rage. It took him outward and inward. "Meditation has become something I cannot do without. I see and hear more clearly, feel more relaxed and calm, and I actually find my experiences slowing down," he wrote in 1997. "I'm more appreciative of each day as I observe how things constantly change and dissolve. I've realized that everything is in a continual process of coming and going. I don't hold happiness or anger for a long time. It just comes and goes."

He's also connected to the outside world through his writing. He's the author of two published books and many magazine essays. He told me that his essays "go out on their own wings and some of them fly back to me." It's not the first time he's used flight as a metaphor for his own reach; the title of his memoir comes from an incident when he stopped another prisoner from nailing a seagull with a basketball in the prison yard. Asked why, he said off the top of his head, "That bird has my wings," and so the gripping, moving narrative of his early years is titled *That Bird Has My Wings*.

"You know, it's really hard to get in," I told Masters, about my attempts to figure out how to move through the prison system and arrive at our visit. "It was easy for me," he replied, and we laughed. From the time I first wrote him, it took me approximately two months of bureaucratic wrangling to be able to visit him. Finally, on a cold Sunday in January, I showed up at the visitors' entrance wearing clothing in the permitted colors and carrying what few articles I was allowed: a key, a state-issued ID, some coins and bills for the vending machines, and a few pages of fact-checker's questions and quotes to verify, sealed inside a clear Ziploc bag. After half an hour in a waiting room inhabited largely by women of color, I showed my ID, was checked against the system's file on me, and passed through an x-ray machine. On the other side, I stepped out to face a shabby jumble of sinister architectural styles. I was suddenly left alone to find my way to the visiting rooms a couple hundred yards away.

There were more doors to go through, operated by a young woman in the guard booth, who let me in and took my license and pass. I entered a room in which everything except the vending machines was painted a pale buttery yellow. There were fifteen cages in which prisoners were locked with their visitors, a U-shaped arrangement with guards on the inside (where prisoners entered) and outside (where the visitors entered). Each cage was about four by seven feet, not much smaller than the cells the prisoners live in, and was furnished with two plastic chairs and a tiny table.

A guard wearing a heavy belt with keys dangling on steel chains locked me in the cage closest to the door through which the prisoners entered and exited. Masters arrived with his hands cuffed behind him. He offered them up through a slot in the cage so the guard could unlock him, a gesture both had apparently engaged in so many times that it appeared utterly routine. Thus began my first face-to-face meeting with Masters. Soon afterward a stocky white man with gray hair passed by on his way out of the visiting room, and he and Masters shouted something at each other. It was a little unclear to me whether this was animosity or friendship, but Masters said it was the latter. The two men had known each other since being in foster care together. It was as though they'd been groomed for death row since they were little boys.

Another prisoner on his way back to his cell stopped to say that his daughter was on break from college and coming to see him. After their conversation and his departure, with the guard watching over him, Masters told me that he'd become a confidant, someone who, because of his writings and the way he conducted himself, was trusted with personal information that prisoners might not ordinarily share. He reminded me that he's been in prison since before some of the younger inmates and guards were born.

"I have been so blessed because I was thinking about all that could have gone wrong, that could've affected me," he told me. "All the things that didn't go wrong. I have seen a lot of tragedy, and all of those things could've been me. I've seen the violent heart, and I count my blessings that I haven't had that kind of hatred. Being on death row, I have a front row seat on what suffering is. I'm not damaged, not had this place tear me up like I've seen a hundred times. I'm probably crazy for not being crazy. I count my blessings every day."

When I started rowing, I thought it would be a meditative practice of sorts, because so much concentration goes into the single gesture that moves you across the water. That repetitive movement requires the orchestration of the whole body, and it contains a host of subtleties in timing and positioning and force. You could spend a lifetime learning to do it right, but even as you're learning you can go miles across the water. Gradually the gestures became second nature, and I could think about other things. Though I don't get lost in thought much. It's too beautiful.

Buddhism calls for the liberation of all beings, and it's a useful set of tools for thinking about prisons and what we do with our freedoms. We are all rowing past one another, and it behooves us to know how the tides move and who's being floated along and who's being dragged down and who might not even be allowed in the water.

I bought Masters some things from the vending machines just outside the cages, which I could access and he couldn't. He asked whether I was going to eat, and I said maybe I'd get a taco after. He said, "That's freedom." He was right. Freedom to eat tacos on my own schedule, to pursue the maximum freedom of rowing, to enter the labyrinth of San Quentin and leave a couple of hours later, to listen to stories and to tell them, to try to figure out which stories might free us.

It was stories written down by Melody Ermachild Chavis, by the Zen priest who's now Jarvis's spiritual guide, Alan Senauke, and by Jarvis Masters himself that made me care about him and think about him and talk to him and visit him. And it was these stories that made me hope to see him leave that cage on his own wings. Meanwhile, there is a way Jarvis is already free; as a storyteller he's escaped the narratives about himself he's been given, and he's made his own version of what a life means.

"Whatever the outcome, I want to be in a position to deal with that," he told me. "There are a lot of people who say, 'Jarvis, you gonna win this case.' It's the same way the other way," meaning people who say he won't win. "I'm scared both ways; I'm scared to think this way and scared that way. Do I lose sleep? Of course, I lose sleep. I do have some faith in this system, I just have to. The possibility of them coming to the right decision is there. I do have faith in the outcome of this system. History doesn't give you a lot of good reasons for it. That's just my bottom line."

◆

CODA: CASE DISMISSED (2016, 2018)

Masters's lawyers filed their opening appeal brief in his case in 2001. On February 22, 2016, the long-awaited California Supreme Court ruling was handed down. It upheld his death penalty conviction and reaffirmed the legitimacy of his trial. That trial included what seem to be arbitrary or biased decisions about who would be regarded as a reliable witness and what evidence was admitted or not admitted.

The appeals process only allows challenges to the content of a trial itself. Now that the appeal has failed—after fifteen years of Masters's life were spent in a small cage under a death sentence—his lawyers have petitioned for a rehearing and will continue with a *habeas corpus* petition. The latter allows new information to be introduced—including the fact that many witnesses recanted—and presents a stronger case overall. Still, whether Masters will ever be exonerated and go free is impossible to guess.

What we do know is that the odds are against him.

They have been against him much of his life. A good deal of space in the seventy-three-page Supreme Court decision is devoted to reciting bad things Masters is said to have done as a minor. One detail the court saw fit to bring up is this: "In 1974, when Masters was 12 years old, he took some change from another boy's pocket, but ultimately gave the money back after the boy pleaded with Masters not to take it. Masters later told police that he had merely borrowed a dime from the boy but returned it when the boy said he wanted it back." The court included this laughably minor exchange as evidence of his immorality, but it tells a story other than what the judges intended, about a child who was already being treated as a criminal, already stuck inside the legal system. (Masters was a foster child from an early age and, after he ran away from a brutal home, an inmate in the juvenile justice system.) Most of us committed petty crimes when we were children; most of us were not interrogated by the police or had it go on our record to be brought up against us forty-two years later.

Masters was supposed to be tried and found innocent or guilty only of playing a role in the murder of a prison guard. But the appellate decision shows how much the state built up a portrait of him as a person guilty of many other things—including being a former member of a Black prison gang whose revolutionary philosophy was also considered relevant. He was, in sum, put on trial as someone who was more or less inherently criminal and inherently dangerous. It's impossible not to consider that his race was a part of this.

The overall impression I came away with from reading the court decision was that he was considered a low-grade person who only deserved a low-grade trial. It's certainly what he got. Another remarkable passage in the California Supreme Court decision states: "Defense counsel sought to examine a correctional officer about various notes found in the prison that claimed responsibility for Sergeant Burchfield's murder. These notes were turned over to the prison's investigators but were apparently lost.... The officer also saw at least 10 other notes claiming responsibility for Sergeant Burchfield's murder. The trial court precluded the officer from testifying about the note." In other words, conflicting evidence was lost, and potentially exonerating testimony was excluded. The California Supreme Court did not have a problem with this. Nor did it have problems with the pivotal testimony of the prosecution's main witness—another member of the same gang, who had been given immunity in exchange for his testimony and who had refused to speak or meet with the defense team. The court decision mentions this and dismisses it, as it does testimony by other prisoners that this key witness was unreliable. He testified to Masters's role in the killing but initially described a man who differed substantially from Masters. The description closely matched another gang member who actually confessed to making the murder weapon, but Masters's lawyers were not at the time told these crucial facts.

Joe Baxter, Masters's lead lawyer, described the court's ruling as "a shabby product" that was "poorly written and poorly reasoned," and said it made factual and legal mistakes. "Justice delayed is justice denied" is an oft-cited legal maxim, and you could apply it to Masters's case; but whether there was ever a chance of justice in the first place is a question worth asking. That a man was condemned to death and has lived in grim conditions for thirty-five years on the basis of shabby evidence and procedures makes "justice" too good a word for what happened to Jarvis Jay Masters.

As of 2018, Joe Baxter was preparing for the habeas corpus hearing. We await its results.

The Monument Wars

(2017)

For years, whenever I was in New Orleans, I used to run past an equestrian statue just outside the voluptuously green City Park. Though it was situated at a major intersection, where Esplanade Avenue meets Wisner Boulevard, the statue itself was unremarkable, the usual muscular horse and male rider. It celebrated Pierre Gustave Toutant Beauregard, the general whose assault on Fort Sumter in April 1861 launched the Civil War. Beneath the horse's raised foreleg, a plaque commemorates the four years that Beauregard served in the Confederate Army; it says nothing about his decades in the US Army. A few miles to the south, at the center of Lee Circle, Beauregard's Confederate commander and fellow slaveholder Robert E. Lee loomed atop a sixty-foot marble column, his arms crossed, a sword at his side. Lee was too high up to be clearly seen, as though purposefully placed out of the reach of anyone who might question why he was there.

Monuments to the South's Confederate past were not hard to find in New Orleans. On the banks of the Mississippi, a white obelisk paid tribute to the 1874 Battle of Liberty Place, a bloody attempt by a racist paramilitary group called the Crescent City White

League to overthrow the Reconstructionist Louisiana government. The administration, which had both Black and white members, was defended by a Black militia as well as by New Orleans police. During the skirmishes, the White League militants used streetcars as barricades and hid behind bales of cotton. A few dozen people died, including eleven policemen. The insurrection was quashed, but its goal of ending Reconstruction was realized within two years, when the presidential election of 1876 rolled back the reforms of the previous decade and disenfranchised Black voters. In 1932, an inscription was added to the monument, praising the overthrow of the "carpetbag government." The national election, the inscription reads," recognized white supremacy and gave us our state."

"Us," of course, refers to white people. The history books insist that the North won the war, but in the South it's hard to find the evidence. If the North had won the war, there would not be statues and street names honoring the defeated leaders. If the North had won the war, our monuments would be to the suffering of slaves and their struggle to be free. If the North had won the war, the Confederate flag would be a symbol of shameful beliefs and military defeat, seen only in museums. If the North had won the war, the war would be over. Or so I thought, coming to the South as an adult unaccustomed to encountering that flag and those monuments as an ordinary part of the civic landscape.

In the West, where I currently live, we have our own unfinished wars: the Indian wars. I was reminded how unfinished they are when I attended a demonstration led by Native Americans against the Dakota Access Pipeline in 2016. The protest took place on the vast greensward in front of the statehouse in Bismarck, North Dakota, where a memorial to pioneers stands. The gray, cast-metal statue depicts a family: a patriarch, his shirt unbuttoned, poised for action; a matriarch, babe in her arms, leaning into her husband; and their strapping son. This is a military monument, despite its domestic subject, one of the many across the West that commemorate the invaders of these lands as heroes and, more than that, as *us*, while insisting that Native Americans are *them*.

That the hundred or more young Native people in that crowd in Bismarck had to face a symbol of their status as the enemy seemed as threatening, in its way, as the long line of heavily armed cops who were there. It was impossible not to think of the US government's military campaigns against the Lakota and Dakota a century and a half ago, which made some— eventually most—of the tribal territory available for white settlement and, of course, for exploitation. Part of the goal was to secure mineral resources. The Indian wars were and are frequently resource wars. North Dakota, like Louisiana and Alberta, has become hostage to oil interests, and the state seems to have declared a new war on its original inhabitants, treating as violent aggressors people who have declared peace and prayer as their tactics. When I visited the Standing Rock reservation, multiple roadblocks stopped people from getting near the activist camps. I was told by government security officers that they were turning people back for their own safety, which seemed to be an attempt to instill fear and portray peaceful resistors as terrorists or criminals.

Plenty of statues in the West depict men who killed and dispossessed indigenous people. But most of the memorials depict what followed the initial invasion and conflict: white settlement. In San Francisco, a pioneer mother with her children overlooks a path in Golden Gate Park; near City Hall towers another, bigger monument, with several groups of bronze figures, including one that shows a Spanish priest and a vaquero standing over a cringing Native American man. They're supposed to be "civilizing" him, but they look more like cops roughing up a suspect.

A city is a book we read by wandering its streets, a text that favors one version of history and suppresses others, enlarges your identity or reduces it, makes you feel important or disposable depending on who you are and what you are. When I called Maurice Carlos Ruffin, a writer and lawyer who lives in New Orleans, to discuss his city's Confederate monuments, he told me, "The statues—a lot of them physically beautiful—argue that if you're white, you're human, and if you're not, you're not." He's not.

Who is remembered, and how? Who decides? These are political questions. "Who controls the past," George Orwell wrote in *1984*, "controls the future." Those in the United States trying to shape the future know this, as well as the rest of Orwell's admonition: "Who controls the present controls the past." We are not who we once were—"we" meaning the citizens of a country whose nonwhite population has grown, in numbers and in visibility and in power, but remains marginalized in countless ways. Racism is so embedded that if we were to cease honoring slaveholders, we would have to rename cities and counties and the state of Washington; sexism is so deeply entrenched that the great women of history are largely missing from our streets and squares. What is to be done with a landscape whose features carry the legacy of violence? Do we tear down what's already standing? Do we work toward parity by erecting new buildings, new monuments? Do we recontextualize or reclaim what is already there?

A quarter century ago, in Birmingham, Alabama, a series of sculptures was erected to commemorate the civil rights movement. The most startling, by the artist James Drake, flanks a pedestrian path in a city park. Emerging from a wall on one side and the ground on the other, snarling bronze and steel dogs lunge as if to tear apart any passersby. The sculpture suggests that to understand the violence people once met with here, we need to experience at least a shadow of that violence ourselves. It's a rare thing, an official memorial to institutional savagery on the site where it transpired.

History, unlike physics, does not have an equal and opposite reaction for every action, but sometimes it has a curious way of advancing. In June 2015, nine Black people were killed inside the Emanuel African Methodist Episcopal Church in Charleston, South Carolina, a city where the Confederate flag is frequently displayed. The bloodbath, which was intended to be the opening salvo of a race war, had the opposite symbolic effect: it forced people to confront the flag's association with racist violence.

The standard defense of the Confederate flag is that it is an emblem of history, but its display in South Carolina doesn't date back to the nineteenth century: it first flew over the statehouse in 1961, ostensibly resurrected to mark the centennial of the Civil War but really as a symbol of opposition to integration. After the Charleston massacre, the activist Bree Newsome scaled a flagpole at the capitol to take it down; she was arrested. A month later, in a milestone marking the road away from Jim Crow, legislators finally ordered it taken down for good.

Across the South, public memory has been shifting—or at least expanding—to acknowledge previously overlooked facets of history. In October 2016, the town of Abbeville, South Carolina, unveiled a monument to a man named Anthony Crawford, a century after a mob beat, tortured, shot, and hanged him for arguing with a white man over the price of his crops. In Montgomery, Alabama, the Equal Justice Initiative is building a memorial to the more than four thousand Black victims of lynching. The city also houses a Rosa Parks museum.

Many of these advances meet with ferocious resistance. In New Orleans, when the obelisk honoring the Crescent City White League was removed, in 1989, from its prime location at the foot of

Canal Street, a follower of David Duke, the Ku Klux Klan grand wizard, led a successful lawsuit to make sure that the landmark at which so many Klan marches had originated remained present and visible in the city. In 1993, it was installed in a less conspicuous location a block away.

In 2014, jazz musician Wynton Marsalis asked Mitch Landrieu, the city's white mayor at the time, to look at the towering statue of General Lee: "Let me help you see it through my eyes. Who is he? What does he represent? And in that most prominent space in the city of New Orleans, does that space reflect who we were, who we want to be, or who we are?"

A year later, the mayor proposed that the city take down the statue, along with others that commemorated the Confederate cause. Then city employees were threatened, and the contractor who accepted the job of removing the statues received death threats and withdrew.

Residents' frustrations over the delay have erupted periodically into outright conflict. In September 2016, Take 'Em Down NOLA, an activist group led by African Americans, began protesting the statue of Andrew Jackson that sits in the heart of the French Quarter. Jackson fought against Native Americans, owned and traded slaves, and signed the Indian Removal Act of 1830, which dispossessed the Cherokee, Choctaw, Seminole, and other southeastern tribes of their lands. The several hundred demonstrators who poured into Jackson Square found that the statue had been placed behind barricades and was being protected by police. Meanwhile, a counterprotest sought to obstruct the activists. When David Duke himself showed up at Jackson Square, a quarrel broke out, and in the scuffle police arrested seven people, including the gray-haired woman who had wrested Duke's megaphone out of his hands.

The statue remained standing, but Duke's followers seemed worried that it was doomed. On Duke's website, a commenter wrote, "To the victor go the spoils—and the ability to humiliate the vanquished. One of the most iconic ways is to destroy the statues and monuments of the defeated side."

He has a point. If you want to see defeat, Berlin might be the best place to look. The city has repudiated its role in the Third Reich with a formidable array of museums, statues, memorials, and other urban aide-mémoire. The most dramatic is the nearly five-acre Memorial to the Murdered Jews of Europe. It's like a city in miniature, a grid of nearly three thousand blank brown concrete plinths, all the same width and depth but of varying heights. It's a city of absence, of wordless commemoration, eerie to walk through. Completed in 2005, it commemorates only Jewish victims of the Holocaust; later memorials rectify the omission with monuments to gay victims and to Roma victims. The former SS headquarters also memorialize genocide. There's a Jewish museum that does so as well.

And then there are the "stumbling blocks"—*Stolperstein* literally means a stone you trip over, and it can also mean something you stumble across, as in discover. The German artist Gunter Demnig has since 1996 laid more than 50,000 small—about four-inch-square—bronze plaques in the streets in front of homes from which victims of the Holocaust were taken, including Jews, Jehovah's Witnesses, Roma, homosexuals, and dissidents. The Stolperstein project continues, according to Demnig's website; with funding from donors and data from the Yad Vashem archives, he is installing about 450 carefully crafted, small, gold-colored memorials a month.

Memory is overtaking oblivion, at least in these small interpolations that must jolt people's sense of time and place when they come across one unexpectedly. They are installed in other cities in

Germany and beyond, a dispersed project to insist that places must have memories, and we must remember what took place in them. Memory, too, can die—or it can be kept alive. And who is remembered, and how, and who decides: these are deeply political things. The physical spaces we inhabit control the past through statues, names, and representations.

In New Orleans, in the places where those monuments still stand, so does the Confederacy. Yet artists and activists are making interventions into public space all over the country, some of them elaborate, some more ad hoc. The insult of the pioneer monument in Bismarck was temporarily solved by draping it with a bed sheet, on which was painted, "Protect Our Mother." In New Orleans, the Jefferson Davis monument was tagged "slave owner" to draw attention to what was left off the plaque. On Memorial Day in 2015, John Sims, a conceptual artist, organized burnings and burials of the Confederate flag in thirteen Southern states. "The Confederate flag is the n-word on a pole," he said. One of the burials took place at Lee Circle.

In periods when progressives don't hold federal power, the work of rights and racial justice is largely relegated to the state and local levels. In the Trump era, this change of focus becomes imperative—if we advance at all, it will be through actions taken in our own communities, on city councils and in neighborhood assemblies and on the streets. The fight is perhaps most powerful, most poignant, when the guerrilla revisionists wage it.

To mark the four-hundredth anniversary of the 1598 arrival of Juan de Oñate, a Spanish colonial governor, a statue was erected north of Santa Fe, New Mexico. In that part of the country, the Native American pueblos are strung like beads along the silver thread of the Rio Grande. Native memory is long, and Oñate had not been forgiven for chopping off the right feet of the Acoma

Pueblo men who rose against him. So one night, several years after its installment, the statue's booted, spurred foot was severed from its leg. In a letter to the editor of the *Albuquerque Journal,* a person who claimed involvement wrote, "If you must speak of his expedition, speak the truth in *all* its entirety."

What is the whole truth? How do we reach it? In the monument wars, as we excavate our history like an archaeological site—or a crime scene—we have a chance to arrive at new conclusions, nominate new heroes, rethink the past, and reorient ourselves to the future. Some classes of people are educated, others rebuked. On occasion, the public dialogue produces something tangible. In Lower Manhattan, a grand statue of George Washington, yet another slaveholder, stands guard over Federal Hall, as it has since 1882. But a few blocks away, in a small counterpoint to the master narrative, a recently installed sign remembers Wall Street's eighteenth-century slave market.

The playing field is level, shout the men on the mountaintop to the people below. From the abyss, the people shout back in disagreement.

Trump's disgraceful genius has been to supply his followers with a simple—and false—account of history, to inflame their nostalgia for an imagined antiquity so as to invite its triumphant return. White nationalists have been empowered by Trump's victory to keep rewriting in this mold, or to erase our revisions. Their falsifications are best resisted not with the substitution of one simple story for another but with the addition of contradictory details, complicating facts. It would be impossible and unwise to erase all signs of the ugliness of this country's past; success would be a landscape lobotomy. And just as we can't forget that our statuary reinforces the exclusions and insults of the present, so should we remember that our emerging perspective is hardly the final realization of inclusion or equality. Posterity will alter or undo our contributions and curse us for crimes we have not yet comprehended. Statues stand still; the culture moves past them.

But then, in May 2017, the four Confederate statues in New Orleans came down. New Orleans had symbolically exited the Confederacy. Many other cities and campuses followed. We have not left the Confederacy behind, but we have joined battle again.

Eight Million
Ways to Belong

October 20, 2016

Dear Donald Trump,

I wonder if you have ever actually explored the New York City you claim to live in. I recommend it, because it has beauties and splendors that undermine so many of the assertions I have heard you make during your campaign, particularly in the final debate. For starters, its eight million–plus population includes a huge percentage of immigrants, Muslims, Blacks, Mexicans, and some lovely people who are Black, Muslim, and immigrant all at once. Only a third of its residents are white. You talk as if should lots of undocumented immigrants and Muslims show up here, there'll be trouble. I have news for you: they're here, and it seems to be working out rather well.

Do you ever come down from your tower, other than to stuff yourself into a limousine en route to a jet? You rail against immigrants, but more than a third of New York City residents are immigrants—37 percent. About five hundred thousand of its residents are undocumented, and they are some of the hardest workers making this city go. If you drove them out, the restaurant and hotel industries would collapse into crisis. Unlike you, 75 percent of un-documented New York City residents pay taxes, according to for-mer mayor Michael Bloomberg, who also points out the low crime rate among that population. Overall, whether they're janitors or doctors, immigrants energize and enrich this city.

You should check out Queens, the borough in which you were raised. It is now the most linguistically diverse place on earth. It's the part of the city where most of the eight hundred languages to be found here are spoken. A lot of the languages here are vanishing tongues, as I learned from one of New York's most enchanting or-ganizations, the Endangered Language Alliance. People come here as refugees and they bring their culture with them. Some of the last speakers of languages from the Himalayas and the Andes are here, and they make this city a world in which many worlds fit, a conver-sation in which many languages belong, and a place of refuge, as it was for my mother's grandparents when they escaped hunger and dis-crimination in Ireland, my father's parents when they passed through Ellis Island, escaping the kind of pogroms you seem to be instigating.

You treat Muslims like dangerous outsiders, but you seem ig-norant of the fact that the town you claim to live in has about 285 mosques, and somewhere between 400,000 and 800,000 Muslims, according to New York's wonderful religious scholar Tony Carnes. That means one out of ten to one out of twenty New Yorkers are practitioners of the Islamic faith. A handful of Muslims—includ-ing the Orlando mass murderer, who was born in Queens—have done bad things, but when you recognize how many Muslims there are, you can stop demonizing millions for the acts of a few.

And that Orlando killer: his homophobia, easy access to guns, history of domestic violence—these are homegrown problems we need to work on, not imports. New York has also led the way in liberating gay, lesbian, and trans people from discrimination, or rather they freed themselves with campaigns, projects, sanctuary spaces, and communities that spread liberation nationwide and beyond. I just had my first drink at the Stonewall Inn in the West Village, and it was a big thrill to be there, where uprisings and resistance shifted the conversation and moved rights forward almost fifty years ago.

But we were talking about Muslims, not gay, lesbian, and trans residents, though I'm sure there are some gay, lesbian, and trans Muslims to include, because everyone is here. Everyone. New York City Muslims are taxi drivers, the guys inside some of the halal food carts all over Manhattan, as well as lawyers and scholars and professors, programmers, and designers. They are fathers, toddlers, grandmothers, high-schoolers. Part of what's so beautiful about this city is how complex the cross-categorizations are. A lot of Muslims are immigrants or children and grandchildren of immigrants, from Africa as well as Asia, but a significant percentage are African Americans, whose roots go far deeper in this country's history than yours or mine do. Their ancestors built this place, including, literally, the wall that Wall Street is named for.

Speaking of African Americans: have you ever *been* to Harlem or the Bronx? You keep talking about Black people like you've never met any or visited any Black neighborhoods. Seriously, during the last debate you said, "Our inner cities are a disaster. You get shot walking to the store. They have no education. They have no jobs. I will do more for African Americans and Latinos than [Clinton] can ever do in ten lifetimes. All she's done is talk to the African Americans and to the Latinos." Dude, seriously? Did you get this sense of things from watching TV—in 1975? New York City has a 70 percent high-school graduation rate, only a bit lower than that for Black and Latinx teens, and about a 5 percent unemployment rate. And by the way, talking to people is a really great way to discover where you are and who they are. You should try it. "Inner cities" is a stale, leftover term from when cities like New York were crumbling from divestment and declining population, and crime really was high (news flash: it's declined nationwide over the past quarter century, even though you like to harp on the hiccup in Chicago). When you talk about the "inner city," you sound about forty years out of date.

Someday you should visit the boomtown that is New York today. Take Harlem, one of the great cultural centers of the United States, the great heart of Black culture in the United States for at least a century, the place where some of this country's greatest writers grew up or ended up. It's full of people with excellent jobs and educations, and to say otherwise is as ignorant as it is racist. It's not a place riddled with crime, unless you want to call gentrification and displacement a crime—which I know you don't, but sometimes I do, when I see how it hacks away at the cultural memory and continuity of a place and targets the vulnerable. But you and I are bound to disagree on real estate speculation, so let's move on.

Seriously, just visit New York. It's huge. It's great. It is, among other things, a great Latin American city. Did you know that the most listened-to radio stations here are in Spanish? That daytime DJ Alex Sensation—a Colombian immigrant—has the top radio show in the top market in the US? His show mixes many kinds of Latin music, because New York is the Latin American capital where everyone's shown up, from Cubans and Dominicans to Colombians to Guatemalans. In this great mix of culture, salsa music evolved and migrated outward, one of the United States' greatest exports, along with hip-hop and rap, born in the South Bronx, now a vital part of popular culture from Inuit Canada to central Africa.

This has been a place of liberation, for the refugees who came here from all over; for the institutions that arose here, like Planned

Parenthood, which you threaten to defund; for groups like Black Lives Matter, which you've denounced. Maybe that's why you haven't visited New York: it doesn't agree with you and it undermines your ideology. There are so many New Yorks, and we all get to choose our own, but the New York of rich white people is a small slice of the city. Beyond it are a thousand New Yorks with thousands of ways of living and working, hundreds of languages, dozens of religions, and it all comes together every day on subway platforms, on the streets, in the parks, the hospitals, the kitchens, the public schools. Because ordinary New Yorkers get out and mix, and this coexistence with difference is the beautiful basis for a truly democratic spirit, a faith that we can trust each other and literally (and figuratively) find common ground by mingling in public.

If you're not ready to get out and mix, here's a very short reading assignment: read some money. Not the big stuff. Look at a dime. It says "e pluribus unum." Out of many, one. That's been one of this country's key mottos since its founding. It's realized in our cities, our great places of coexistence. Not just a tolerance of difference, but a delight in it, love for it, cross-pollination, intermarriage, hybridization, and the invention of new forms from the differences we bring with us as we come together. That's a lot of what makes America great when it is great and not angry, divisive, unequal, and deluded. And it's right here, all around us, in the big city.

Sincerely,
Rebecca Solnit

The Light
from Standing Rock
(2016)

No one saw it coming. Suddenly, on Sunday, December 4, 2016, word went out that the US Army Corps of Engineers was withdrawing permission to build the Dakota Access Pipeline (DAPL) under the Missouri River, just above the Standing Rock Sioux reservation. What do you do with a victory? A lot of people on social media cautioned everyone that this was not the total final Santa-is-real, everything-is-okay-forever victory, and we should not celebrate. If we waited for that, we'd never celebrate anyway. But the people most involved seemed to get it that this is a really nice chapter, not the end of the story, and you can celebrate that chapter. Which people did, with all kinds of hoopla and merriment at Standing Rock and around the world.

It is not a final victory. Donald Trump is doing his best to make sure that this and every other pipeline is built. That's a given at this point. But it might be a really big victory.

The Institute for Energy Economics and Financial Analysis notes, in a study issued in November 2016, "The broader economic context for the project has changed radically since ETP [Energy Transfer Partners] first proposed it, in 2014. Global oil prices began to collapse just a few months after shippers committed to using DAPL, and market forecasters do not expect prices to regain 2014 levels for at least a decade. As a result, production in the Bakken Shale oil field has fallen for nearly two consecutive years." The profit in the pipeline was to come from shippers who were locked into 2014 prices if the project was completed by January 1, 2017.

Which this gift from the US Army Corps makes quite unlikely. It's a big blow. The report concludes, "If production continues to fall, DAPL could well become a stranded asset—one that was rushed to completion largely to protect favorable contract terms negotiated in 2014." That's really nice news if you're not an investor, and news that amplifies the significance of the victory.

There's a lot to learn from the beautiful struggle at Standing Rock, though everyone will draw their own conclusions. Mine include the importance of knowing that we don't know what will happen next and have to live on principles, hunches, and lessons from history. Plenty of people made pronouncements about what was going to happen and what would never happen at Standing Rock that turned out to be wrong. No one saw this coming.

Another is standing up for what you believe in, even when victory seems remote to impossible. Sunday, December 4, was the pipeline victory. The next day was the sixty-first anniversary of the beginning of the Montgomery Bus Boycott. What did those African Americans living under Jim Crow hope for? Surely more than integrating the public transit system. They could not have assumed that they would help launch a movement that not only changed the nation and led to national legislation, but also offered a toolbox of nonviolent strategies and visions to the world, used in South Africa and Egypt, in Czechoslovakia and the Philippines. But they bet that the future would be different than the past and did everything to make it so. This is a moment when the civil rights movement's victories seem to be in jeopardy—but that is all the more reason to remember that they were victories, and they were achieved in blood and pain and dedication when victory was far from sight.

And that's another thing that matters. Consequences are often indirect. The movement at Standing Rock may yet stop a pipeline. Whether it does or not, it has brought together perhaps the greatest single gathering of Native North Americans (from Canada as well as the United States) ever, and that has been a profound and moving watershed for the growth of a transnational network of solidarity, the affirmation of cultural identities and political rights. It has demonstrated yet again that the environmental movement and human rights campaigns are often inseparable; reminded us that, worldwide, indigenous people are at the forefront of the climate movement, and that many nonnative people respect and look for leadership from these cultures. Many things we cannot foresee may come of this gathering and its vision, tactics, and power.

In this moment of right-wing and white-supremacist triumphalism, we are hearing a lot about hate crimes: beatings, insults, swastikas, threats, and more. But also rising into view is another America, with another set of beliefs, the people who stand up for racial justice, for the vulnerable, for women and LGBTQ people, for science, and for democracy. You can see it in the capital neighborhood that greeted relocating vice president Mike Pence with rainbow flags, with the defenders of the persecuted, and with the enormous desire to protect people, places, values, democracy itself. This is a turbulent moment, and in it much is possible. Standing Rock prefigured and modeled those possibilities and was radiant with this beauty.

I went to Standing Rock in early September 2016, when the weather was delightful and the landscape green. While there, I asked Dallas Goldtooth of the Indigenous Environmental Network what were the precedents for this. Sitting in the back of his mini-van, as his small children milled about and the boy across the road came to shake his hand, he told me: "There's nothing, honestly. There's nothing that can compare. One hundred and eighty differ-ent tribal nations have sent letters of solidarity." Goldtooth, who is Dakota and Dene, went on to describe the unprecedented support of tribes from all over the United States and Canada for this resist-ance, along with climate and environmental groups—a coalition with tremendous possibility for the future of both indigenous rights and the climate movement.

The joy is widespread. The first person I met when I arrived was a young Hoopa/Yurok woman from far-northern California, who told me this is the most amazing thing she's ever been part of. The next morning, a small man came up and greeted me, introduced himself as Frank, "from right here," a member of the Standing Rock Sioux. Somewhere in the conversation he said, "I wake up happy every day about this." I asked him how this changed the past, thinking of the losses the Lakota/Sioux faced over the past 150 years, but he heard the question differently. He mentioned that their old enemies the Crow and the Cheyenne came to stand with them, and that the old divisions are over. When I asked that ques-tion, I was thinking about what I heard from climate activist and environmental lawyer Carolyn Raffensperger, who had spent time at the camp earlier and has a long history in the area. "There are moments in history that can heal the past and the future," she said.

The people who persevered into the brutal winter that followed were heroic, caring more about ideals than comfort, the well-be-ing of the river, tribal rights, and principles than personal safety. It was a noble effort in every sense, guided by prayer, committed to peace, and in it for the long run, come what may. And then came thousands of veterans to stand against the authorities and with the Indians. Then came the Army Corps of Engineers decision.

Standing Rock reminds us, finally, that we are very powerful when we come together to defend our ideals, sometimes only in indirect ways—modeling the possibilities, providing hope and moral reinforcement for what comes later or elsewhere. Sometimes in direct ways, when we remake history.

Five centuries into the dispossession and dehumanization of Native North Americans, this moment when four thousand veterans of the US military came to stand with them, when they won something big, when the world's eyes were turned to one of those places where crimes and depredations are too often invisible: it mattered. As it did when the veterans formally apologized for the depredations of the US Army and asked for forgiveness. And on December 4, the people there and those protesting in banks, writing letters, sending donations, organizing marches around the country, won something worth celebrating. We are facing a lot of trouble on all fronts. Standing Rock reminds us to come together and stand up to it.

IV.
Possibilities

Break the Story

(2016)[1]

"Break the story" is a line journalists use to mean getting a scoop, being the first to tell something, but for me the term has deeper resonance. When you report on any event, no matter how large or small—a presidential election, a school board meeting—you are supposed to come back with a story about what just happened. But, of course, stories surround us like air; we breathe them in, we breathe them out. The art of being fully conscious in personal life means seeing the stories and becoming their teller, rather than letting them be the unseen forces that tell you what to do. Being a public storyteller requires the same skills with larger consequences and responsibilities, because your story becomes part of that water, undermining or reinforcing the existing stories. Your job is to report on the story on the surface, the contained story, the one that happened yesterday. It's also to see and sometimes to break open or break apart the ambient stories, the stories that are already written, and to understand the relationship between the two.

---

1. This is a revised version of a commencement speech at my alma mater, the Graduate School of Journalism at the University of California, Berkeley.

There are stories beneath the stories and around the stories. The recent event on the surface is often merely the hood ornament on the mighty social engine that is a story driving the culture. We call those "dominant narratives" or "paradigms" or "memes" or "metaphors we live by" or "frameworks." However we describe them, they are immensely powerful forces. And the dominant culture mostly goes about reinforcing the stories that are the pillars propping it up and that, too often, are also the bars of someone else's cage. They are too often stories that should be broken, or are already broken and ruined and ruinous and way past their expiration date. They sit atop mountains of unexamined assumptions. Why does the media obediently hype terrorism, which kills so few people in the United States, and mostly trivialize domestic violence, which terrorizes millions of US women over extended periods and kills about a thousand a year? How do you break the story about what really threatens us and kills us?

One thing to keep in mind is the life cycle and food chain of stories. The new stories, the stories that break the story, tend to emerge from the margins and the edges. Gandhi didn't actually say, "First they ignore you, then they laugh at you, then they fight you, then you win," but that's how activism generally works. And when activism wins, it's because, at least in part, the story has become the new narrative, the story the mainstream accepts. Journalism plays a crucial role in this. You can see Black Lives Matter changing the story in our time by shedding light on the epidemic of police killings and the way those killings of young people of color exclude whole communities from their rights—including the right to be protected, not menaced, by public officials. You see how activists took this story known in the Black community, got it to catch fire on social media and get picked up by the news media, which gave extensive coverage to stories that might otherwise have been a little note in the back pages rather than hotly debated national news. We know their names now: Eric Garner, Mario Woods, Walter Scott, Sandra Bland, Tamir Rice, and so many others. The story has been carried from the edges to the center, and people who are not affected directly have gotten on board with those who are.

Part of the job of a great storyteller is to examine the stories that underlie the story you're assigned, maybe to make them visible, and sometimes to break us free of them. Break the story. Breaking is a creative act as much as making, in this kind of writing.

Lots of writers have mooned around, saying that the world is made out of stories as though this is a lovely thing, but it's only as lovely as the stories. There are stories that demonize female anger and Black anger and revere white male rage. There are stories about the inevitability of capitalism, stories that there are two sides to the reality of climate change, a host of stories that don't get told because they rock the boat, discomfort the powerful, unsettle the status quo. Those are stories that will make you wildly unpopular with some people it's great to be wildly unpopular with—and beloved by others it's even greater to be beloved by.

In 2005, a triple disaster struck New Orleans. The hurricane was the least of it; the failure of infrastructure and decades of bad planning and worse implementation made it an accurately predicted, largely manmade disaster, deepened by the failure of the social contract. Poor people were left behind to drown or suffer. Then the mass media showed up to criminalize people trying to survive and obsessed about the possibility that someone was stealing a TV set, making it clear that they considered protecting TV sets more important than rescuing dying grandmothers and traumatized toddlers. They fell back on a clutch of clichés that were already well-established when the 1906 earthquake happened in San Francisco.

By luck of timing, I was fairly well equipped to be skeptical
about the narratives of mobs of raping, looting, murdering humans
gone savage. I had just completed some research and writing on the
1906 earthquake. Those urban legends weren't true in 1906 and
they weren't true in 2005, even though the *Guardian*, *New York
Times*, *Washington Post*, NBC, CBS, CNN, and many other media
outlets reported them. "They tend to travel in herds and report the
same story," Adam Hochschild recently said of journalists in the
Spanish Civil War.

For the tenth anniversary of the manmade catastrophe called
Katrina, I wrote:

> A vast population of mostly African American New Orlea-
> nians was trapped on rooftops, elevated freeways, and in the
> Convention Center and Superdome in the sweltering 80 per-
> cent underwater city, demonized by government and main-
> stream media as too savage and dangerous to rescue or allow
> to leave the city. Would-be rescuers from outside were turned
> back by officials, as were people attempting to flee from inside.
> New Orleans had, at the hand of malevolent authorities, be-
> come a prison. Given how the people of Baltimore were de-
> monized for rising up last April [2015], and how chain stores
> and a predatory check-cashing outlet suddenly became the
> holiest of holy sites for many Americans, it's easy to imagine
> another disaster like it.
>
> The unindicted coconspirator in the dehumanization,
> imprisonment, and death of so many people, mostly African
> Americans, many of them elderly, in New Orleans was and
> is the mainstream media. They fell back on the usual disaster
> stories about looting, raping, marauding hordes, eager to de-
> monize Black people as monsters who were enemies rather
> than as the vulnerable, needy victims of a catastrophe. They
> invented new stories that turned out to be entirely baseless
> about people shooting at helicopters and great piles of corpses
> from imaginary bloodbaths in the Superdome.

To me, those were broken stories, or stories that needed to be broken. I realized, as I kept returning to New Orleans after Katrina, that there had in fact been horrific crimes, and the armies of reporters swamping the city had utterly avoided them or been unable to see them. These were the crimes not of the underclass against the status quo, but of the status quo against the underclass: killings by police and crimes by white vigilantes. I gathered up sources and contacts, photographs and leads, scraps that had been hidden in plain sight, and gave them over to a truly great investigative journalist, A. C. Thompson, who took the material and ran with it. He originated other stories when he got to New Orleans, notably on the police murder of Henry Glover, an unarmed Black man shot in the back. That story sent policemen to prison, something that rarely happens. I did some more reporting myself and wrote a book about how people actually behave in disaster, *A Paradise Built in Hell*.

At some point in this process, I was leaving a radio station, where I'd been talking about what really happened in Hurricane Katrina's aftermath. I turned on my own car radio to hear A. C. talking about the same thing on another station. Sitting there, I thought: we actually broke that story, turned the official version inside out and upside down. The history people remembered ten years later was not the story the mainstream media used to smear poor Black people, and human nature generally, in 2005. We didn't do it alone, of course. Breaking a story is usually a prolonged, collaborative process. It usually begins with activists, witnesses, whistleblowers, and with victims, the people affected, the people on the front lines, the people to whom the story happened. The next step is often carried out by people with storytelling powers who are willing to listen. No journalist is the first person to know anything, if you're reporting on what happened to another person, though, you might be the first person to listen. It's always someone else's story first, and it never stops being their story, either, no matter how well you tell it, how widely you spread it.

In March 2016, one of the great journalists of our time, Ben Bagdikian, died. He broke the story on the tremendous threat to democracy posed by media monopolies, back when I was his student at the UC Berkeley Graduate School of Journalism. Long before that, he was the journalist Daniel Ellsberg trusted to receive the Pentagon Papers, which exposed four presidents' lies about the war in Vietnam and broke the story about the war. I was lucky to be in his class on ethics, where he taught us, "You can't be objective, but you can be fair." *Objective* is a fiction that there is some neutral ground, some political no man's land you can hang out in, you and the mainstream media. Even what you deem worthy to report and whom you quote is a political decision. We tend to treat people on the fringe as ideologues and those in the center as neutral, as though the decision not to own a car is political and the decision to own one is not, as though to support a war is neutral and to oppose it is not. There is no apolitical, no sidelines, no neutral ground; we're all engaged.

"Advocacy journalism" is often used as an incriminating term, but almost any good exposé is advocacy. If you're exposing a president's lies, as Bagdikian and Ellsberg did, you probably think presidents shouldn't lie; if you're exposing a corporation's contamination of the water table—by fracking, say—you're probably not in favor of poisoning, or at least you're in favor of people knowing. It's surprising how many people will defend poisoning people, animals, and places, usually by denying that poison is poisonous or that we have a right to know what toxins are out there. This makes being against poisoning a controversial position at times.

The writer's job is not to look through the window someone else built, but to step outside, to question the framework, or to dismantle the house and free what's inside, all in service of making visible what was locked out of the view. News journalism focuses on what changed yesterday rather than asking what are the underlying forces and who are the unseen beneficiaries of this moment's status quo. A policeman shoots a Black person: What do you need to know, beyond the specifics, to understand the incident, in terms of how often this happens, or how it affects communities and individuals in the long term, or what the usual justifications are? This is why you need to know your history, even if you're a journalist rather than a historian. You need to know the patterns to see how people are fitting the jumble of facts into what they already have: selecting, misreading, distorting, excluding, embroidering, distributing empathy here but not there, remembering this echo or forgetting that precedent.

Some of the stories we need to break are not exceptional events, they're the ugly wallpaper of our everyday lives. For example, there's a widespread belief that women lie about being raped, not a few women, not an anomalous woman, but women in general. This framework comes from the assumption that reliability and credibility are as natural to men as mendacity and vindictiveness are to women. In other words, feminists just made it all up, because otherwise we'd have to question a really big story whose nickname is patriarchy. But the data confirms that people who come forward about being raped are, overall, telling the truth (and that rapists tend to lie, a lot). Many people have gotten on board with the data, many have not, and so behind every report on a sexual assault is a battle over the terms in which we tell, in what we believe about gender and violence.

Every bad story is a prison; breaking the story breaks someone out of prison. It's liberation work. It matters. It changes the world. Percy Bysshe Shelley famously noted that poets are the true legislators of the world; journalists are the story-breakers whose work often changes the belief systems that then drive legislative and institutional change. It's powerful, honorable, profoundly necessary work when it's done with passion and independence and guts. What made *Spotlight* such a great movie was not that it showed how a team of investigative reporters at the *Boston Globe* broke a story about widespread sexual abuse by Catholic priests. It was that the film also showed how the *Globe* had long turned away from breaking the story because it meant shattering comfortable relationships and beliefs.

I think of the mainstream media as having not so much a rightwing or leftwing bias but a status quo bias, a tendency to believe people in authority, to trust institutions and corporations and the rich and powerful and pretty much any self-satisfied white man in a suit; to let people who have been proven to tell lies tell more lies that get reported without questioning; to move forward on cultural assumptions that are readily disproven; and to devalue nearly all outsiders, whether they're discredited or mocked or just ignored. Thus the smoothing over of the transformation of our economy into something far more inequitable over the past third of a century; thus the many major media outlets that went along with the pretense that Iraq had something to do with Al Qaeda and 9/11; thus the long, craven pretense that climate denial funded by fossil fuel corporations represented a legitimate position to be given equal coverage with the consensus of the great majority of qualified scientists.

For journalists and for human beings generally, the elephant in the room has been there for a long time. It's not even the elephant: the elephant in the room is the room itself, the biosphere in which all life currently known to exist in the universe is enclosed, and on which it all depends, the biosphere now devastated by climate change, with far more change to come. The scale is not like anything human beings have faced and journalists have reported on, except perhaps the threat of all-out nuclear war—and that was something that might happen, not something that is happening. Climate change is here, and it is changing everything. It is bigger than anything else, because it *is* everything, for the imaginable future.

Inhabited parts of the earth will become uninhabitable; crop failures are rising, and they create famine, climate refugees, and conflict (climate played a role in the Syrian civil war); the Greenland ice sheet is melting in collapses and torrents; the Western Antarctic ice sheet is also melting far faster than predicted by models a few years ago; sea levels will rise so dramatically by the end of this century that every world atlas will be obsolete and we will have entirely new coastlines in the low-lying places; much of New York City is likely to be doomed in the long run, as is a lot of Bangladesh, Egypt, and Vietnam, along with southern Florida and other parts of the Atlantic seaboard; the oceans are turning into acid baths; the coral reefs that serve as nurseries for fish that feed a significant portion of the earth's human beings are dying rapidly; extinction is accelerating; and turbulent weather is going to be the new normal, producing catastrophes like the spring 2016 mega-fire in Alberta, the biggest disaster in Canadian history (one that was, incidentally, appallingly underreported in the United States), or 2017's catastrophic fires and hurricanes.

All this news has a hard time competing with whatever fleeting human drama best sows righteous indignation and harvests clicks. This is partly the failure of human nature, but partly the failure of the media to put things in perspective and to report on the scale and menace of climate change's impact—and on the shrinking option to minimize rather than maximize it. The stories that we are destroying our home, mostly by slow-moving, indirect, complex means, are largely overlooked and underplayed. Since it's an ongoing process instead of something that erupted yesterday, it's hard to get coverage at all, even when it's "normal news": scandals, lies, and money, as with the concealment by Exxon and other fossil fuel corporations of their awareness of climate change before it was widely reported on or recognized. The magnificent global climate movement and the remarkably swift and effective energy transitions under way are described in fragments when they're discussed at all.

Future generations are going to curse most of us for distracting ourselves with trivialities as the planet burned. Journalists are in a pivotal place when it comes to the possibilities and the responsibilities in this crisis. We, the makers and breakers of stories, are tremendously powerful.

So please, break the story.

Hope in Grief

(2018)

I find great hope and encouragement in the anxiety, fury, and grief of my fellow residents of the United States. It's not that I'm eager to see people suffer but that I'm relieved that so many are so far from indifferent. I feared after the election that those of us who are not directly targeted would do what people have often done during despotic regimes: withdraw into private life, wait it out, take care of themselves and no one else.

Something else happened instead.

The distress is profound. People report deep emotional distress and trouble sleeping, anxiety, preoccupation, rage, rage fatigue, misery, fear, dread, and other emotions—and an obsessive preoccupation with the news. Amy Siskind, a former Wall Street executive, has focused full time on documenting the slide toward authoritarianism with a weekly list of the Trump Administration's transgressive and disturbing actions and statements. She reported in November that she had started wearing a mouth guard at night because she was clenching her jaw in her sleep and had cracked a tooth. An art teacher tells me, "The stress of living in a society that is in very real danger of collapsing into chaos and potential widespread violence is definitely affecting me physically. I feel like I have a mild case of some flu. My thoughts are foggy with heartache. Something tells me that millions of people are feeling this way."

People care. Not everyone is engaged, and of course about a third of the country still supports Trump and wants to return to a semi-imaginary America when white men controlled everything, women were silent, nonwhite people were subservient, heterosexuality was obligatory, and environmental destruction was unregulated. But Gloria Steinem, the eighty-three-year-old feminist and activist, said at an event earlier this year in San Francisco that she has never seen the level of engagement across the country, not in the 1960s, not ever, that she sees around her now. What I see in many lives around me is a passionate concern about principles, about honor, about the vulnerable, about the future, about the rule of law, about the integrity of the institutions on which the nation depends.

Which is to say, they are, we are, idealists. We are public-minded. We are engaged members of society. This goes against what we in the US have been told in every possible way all our lives, and what those of you elsewhere who also live under capitalism, social Darwinism, and what maybe we could call Freudianism have been told: that a human being is a selfish animal concerned with meeting its own bodily and emotional and material needs and perhaps perpetuating its genes, that our desires are private and personal. Indeed, during the rise of corporate globalization and the transnational anti-globalization movement, I often noted that before you privatized a bank or a railroad you had to privatize imaginations and convince people that we do not have anything in common with each other that matters; that we owe each other nothing; that our lives are ideally lived out in domestic and personal arenas; that we are consumers, not citizens; that there is no reason we should want to live in public or participate in public life. It has worked in many ways. We are told over and over that the public sphere is superfluous, messy, unpleasant, dangerous, not where our pleasures and purpose are located, and Silicon Valley has worked hard to profit off this point of view.

And yet in crises, as I found out when I studied disasters such as earthquakes and hurricanes, people often revert spontaneously to a more communitarian sense of self, and in that deeper connection find meaning, purpose, power—and sometimes even joy amid the ruins. I have often thought, over the past fifteen months or so, that part of how we know this is a crisis, a disaster, an emergency is in the way people have shaken themselves awake to respond. People find that they are members of civil society, that they care about strangers and about the collective good, that they will sometimes change or risk their lives for these things, and that their sense of self expands as they move into a more public and collective arena.

I feared after the election that people would be intimidated into public deference and private indifference. After 9/11 the Bush administration skillfully manipulated the event and the response to make patriotism a sort of blind obedience from which few dared dissent in the years after. One of the joys of this ugly era is that hardly anyone seems to fear the Trump administration; his every tweet is greeted with a host of responses by ordinary people that range from mockery to scorn to denunciation as a criminal. In fact, if anything protects this country from going full-scale authoritarian, it is the insubordinate nature of so many of the people here, as well as their commitment to the principles that this country has often declared but just as often has failed to adhere to.

It is not enough to oppose tyranny and corruption in your heart, to feel distress, to care. You have to act. But those feelings are a foundation, and real, practical opposition is all around us. Hundreds of women are running for elected office for the first time and winning, and Democrats are winning in traditionally Republican districts, because of massive engagement on the part of voters who do not agree with Trump and the Republican Party. (The Democratic Party is, obviously, far from perfect, but it is the main alternative to the deranged far-right Republican Party, and many of the individual candidates are more progressive and more courageous than the party leadership.)

In the spring of 2018 the *Washington Post* reported:

> One in five Americans have protested in the streets or participated in political rallies since the beginning of 2016. Of those, 19 percent said they had never before joined a march or a political gathering. Overwhelmingly, recently motivated activists are critical of Trump. Thirty percent approve of the president, and 70 percent disapprove, according to the poll. And many said they plan to be more involved politically this year, with about one-third saying they intend to volunteer or work for a 2018 congressional campaign.

There is no precedent for this level of engagement.

The high school students of Parkland, Florida, who survived the Valentine's Day 2018 massacre at their school, brought new energy and constituencies into the gun-control movement. A million students are said to have walked out of their classes on March 14, the one-month anniversary of the massacre in that high school. Well over a million took part in more than 450 demonstrations across the country ten days later, on March 24, in the event dubbed March for Our Lives. The Crowd Counting Consortium reports that there were more than 2,500 political demonstrations in the US in one month this spring. The feminist response to the October 2018 revelations about movie producer Harvey Weinstein's sexual harassment and assault has led to the outing and firing of many men like him, and some of the fury may be a side-effect of having a serial sexual assailant in the White House. Both the feminist and anti-gun activists seem to recognize that the particulars are connected to broader questions about power, authority, gender, race, and equality or its opposite.

Labor and education are under attack, but underpaid teachers organized a successful strike in the impoverished state of West Virginia; Oklahoma teachers are now also on strike, as of this writing; and educators in Arizona and North Carolina have struck as well. There are individual campaigns—a fight to protect an immigrant man in Kansas, for example—that people have passionately joined. A strong fight for voting rights has been launched (part of why Trump won his minority victory was the suppression of millions of votes, thanks to an ongoing Republican strategy to win by warring on democracy).

I am not convinced we are winning, but I am glad we are at last fighting. Some of us. It's a chaotic time, as some old-fashioned conservatives take aim at the Trump administration and sometimes even at a Republican Party they feel no longer represents them, and some hardliner leftists are sidelined by their disdain for electoral politics and their lack of faith that better arrangements are possible. Liberals and moderates subscribe passionately to those values, and this may be their finest hour. They are the backbone of what gets called the Resistance.

Sometimes the state of our union seems like an absurdist thriller film that we would not have believed was possible, let alone likely, let alone real, had we been told about it a couple of years ago. That a dignified federal civil servant from a privileged New England background and an adult entertainment actress and director from the Deep South—Robert Mueller III and Stormy Daniels—are together laying siege to the citadel of the Trump administration is both hilarious and terrifying and unbelievably weird.

One complicating factor is that this administration has been in effect a slow-motion coup, in how it gained power and how it exercises power, violating the rule of law and the standards of the office a little and then a little more and a little more, profiting and wrecking as they go. The White House and cabinet conduct themselves as a hostile outside force bent on breaking the public educational system and crushing support for the vulnerable (including the poor, the disabled, children, students, immigrants and refugees, trans people), the diplomatic corps and the bureaucracies that keep this country running, the protections for the American people and the environment, the separation of powers, and the accountability and transparency of government.

They came to destroy, and they are well along with the project, with the help of the Republicans of the legislative branch who apparently no longer care about the law, the truth, or the well-being of the country. Some fear that the administration will suddenly seize power and declare an unchecked authoritarian regime; others note that this has been happening gradually. Two factors countering the attempt are the chaotic incompetence of the Trump administration and the watchful outrage of the general public. A third might be the revulsion of longtime government employees in many sectors, from the military to the intelligence community to the scientists and administrators across the nation. An immigration official resigned in 2018, saying, "I quit because I didn't want to perpetuate misleading facts."

The sorrow and fury, the sleeplessness and indignation, are not in themselves powers, but they testify to a public-spirited population that may be able to take back a country stolen by a corrupted election and unpunished violations of law. And the moment may soon come when we must try.

In Praise of
Indirect Consequences

(2017)

In February 2017, Daniel Ellsberg and Edward Snowden had a public conversation about democracy, transparency, whistleblowing, and more. In the course of it, Snowden—who was, of course, Skyping in from Moscow—said that without Ellsberg's example he would not have done what he did to expose the extent to which the National Security Agency (NSA) was spying on millions of ordinary people. It was an extraordinary declaration. It meant that the consequences of Ellsberg's release of the top-secret Pentagon Papers in 1971 were not limited to the impact on a presidency and a war in the 1970s. The consequences were not limited to people alive at that moment. His act was to have an impact on people decades later—Snowden was born twelve years after Ellsberg risked his future for the sake of his principles. Actions often ripple far beyond their immediate objective, and remembering this is a reason to live by principle and act in the hope that what you do matters, even when results are unlikely to be immediate or obvious.

The most important effects are often the most indirect. I

sometimes wonder when I'm at a mass march, like the January 2017 Women's March, whether the reason it matters is because some unknown young person is going to find her purpose in life that will only be evident to the rest of us when she changes the world in twenty years, when she becomes a great liberator.

I began talking about hope in 2003, in the bleak days after the war in Iraq was launched. Fifteen years later, I still use the term because it navigates a way forward between the false certainties of optimism and of pessimism, and the complacency or passivity that goes with both. Optimism assumes that all will go well without our effort; pessimism assumes it's all irredeemable; both let us stay home and do nothing. Hope for me has meant a sense that the future is unpredictable, and that we don't actually know what will happen, but know we may be able to write it ourselves.

Hope is a belief that what we do might matter, an understanding that the future is not yet written. It's an informed, astute open-mindedness about what can happen and what role we might play in it. Hope looks forward but draws its energies from the past, from knowing histories, including our victories, and their complexities and imperfections. It means not fetishizing the perfect that is the enemy of the good, not snatching defeat from the jaws of victory, not assuming you know what will happen when the future is unwritten, and part of what happens is up to us.

We are complex creatures. Hope and anguish can coexist within us and in our movements and analyses. There's a scene in the 2017 documentary about James Baldwin *I Am Not Your Negro* in which Robert Kennedy predicts, in 1968, that in forty years there will be a Black president. It's an astonishing prophecy, as Barack Obama won the presidential election exactly four decades later, but Baldwin jeers at the comment because the way Kennedy has presented it does not acknowledge that even the most magnificent pie in the sky might comfort white people who don't like racism but doesn't wash away the pain and indignation of Black people suffering that racism in the here and now. Patrisse Cullors, one of the founders of Black Lives Matter, early on described the movement's mission as "rooted in grief and rage but pointed towards vision and dreams." The vision of a better future doesn't have to deny the crimes and sufferings of the present; it matters because of them.

I have been moved and thrilled and amazed by the strength, breadth, depth, and generosity of the resistance to the Trump administration and its agenda. I did not anticipate anything so bold, so pervasive, something that would include state governments, many government employees—from governors and mayors to workers in many federal departments—small towns in red states, new organizations like the six thousand chapters of the grassroots organizing group Indivisible reportedly formed since the election, new and fortified immigrant rights groups, religious groups, one of the biggest demonstrations in US history with the Women's March on January 21, 2017, and so much more.

I've also been worried whether it will endure. Newcomers often think that results are either immediate or they're nonexistent. That if you don't succeed straight away, you failed. Such a framework makes many give up and go back home just when the momentum is building and victories are within reach. This is a dangerous mistake I've seen over and over. To see where we are, you need a complex calculus of change instead of the simple arithmetic of short-term cause and effect.

There's a bookshop I love in Manhattan, the Housing Works Bookstore Cafe, which I've gone to for years for a bite to eat and a superb selection of used books. In fall 2016, my friend Gavin Browning, who works at Columbia University and volunteers with Housing Works, reminded me what the name means. Housing

Works is a spinoff of ACT UP, the Aids Coalition to Unleash Power, founded at the height of the AIDS crisis to push for access to experimental drugs, bring awareness to the direness of the epidemic, and not go gentle into that bad night of premature death.

What did ACT UP do? The group of furious, fierce activists, many of them dangerously ill and dying, changed how we think about AIDS. They pushed to speed up drug trials, deal with the many symptoms and complications of AIDS together, pushed on policy, education, prevention, outreach, funding. They taught people with AIDS and their allies in other countries how to fight the drug companies for affordable access to what they needed. And win.

Browning recently wrote: "At the start of the 1990s, New York City had less than 350 units of housing set aside for an estimated 13,000 homeless individuals living with HIV/AIDS. In response, four members of the ACT UP housing committee founded Housing Works in 1990." They still quietly provide a broad array of services, including housing, to HIV-positive people all these years later.

All I saw was a bookstore; I missed a lot. ACT UP's work is not over, in any sense.

For many groups, movements, and uprisings, there are spinoffs, daughters, domino effects, chain reactions, new models and examples and templates and toolboxes that emerge from the experiments, and every round of activism is an experiment whose results can be applied to other situations. To be hopeful, we need not only to embrace uncertainty but also to be willing to know that the consequences may be immeasurable, may still be unfolding, may be as indirect as poor people on other continents getting access to medicine because activists in the United States stood up and refused to accept things as they were. Think of hope as a banner woven from those gossamer threads, from a sense of the interconnectedness of all things, from the lasting effect of the best actions, not only the worst. Of an indivisible world in which everything matters.

Occupy Wall Street was mocked and described as chaotic and ineffectual in its first weeks; then, when it had spread nationwide and beyond, as failing or failed, by pundits who had simple metrics of what success should look like. The original occupation in lower Manhattan was broken up in November 2011, but many of the encampments inspired by it lasted far longer. Occupy launched a movement against student debt and opportunistic for-profit colleges; it shed light on the pain and brutality of the financial collapse and the American debt-peonage system. It called out economic inequality in a new way. California passed a homeowner's bill of rights to push back at predatory lenders; a housing defense movement arose in the wake of Occupy that, house by house, protected many vulnerable homeowners. Each Occupy had its own engagement with local government and its own projects. The thriving off-shoots of local Occupies still make a difference. Occupy persists, but you have to learn to recognize the myriad forms in which it does so, none of which look much like Occupy Wall Street as a crowd in a square in lower Manhattan.

Similarly, I think it's a mistake to regard the gathering of tribes and activists at Standing Rock, North Dakota, as something we can measure by whether or not it defeated a pipeline. You could go past that to note that merely delaying completion beyond January 1, 2017, cost the investors a fortune, and that the tremendous movement that has generated widespread divestment and a lot of scrutiny of hitherto invisible corporations and environmental destruction makes building pipelines look like a riskier, potentially less profitable business.

Standing Rock was vaster than these practical things. At its height it was almost certainly the biggest political gathering of

Native North Americans ever seen, said to be the first time all seven bands of the Lakota had come together since they defeated Custer at Little Bighorn in 1876, one that made an often-invisible nation visible around the world. What unfolded there seemed as though it might not undo one pipeline but write a radical new chapter to a history of more than five hundred years of colonial brutality, centuries of loss, dehumanization, and dispossession. Thousands of veterans came to defend the encampment and help prevent the pipeline. In one momentous ceremony, many of the former soldiers knelt down to apologize and ask forgiveness for the US Army's long role in oppressing Native Americans. Like the Native American occupation of Alcatraz Island from 1969 to 1971, Standing Rock has been a catalyst for a sense of power, pride, destiny. It is an affirmation of solidarity and interconnection, an education for people who didn't know much about Native rights and wrongs, an affirmation for Native people who often remember history in passionate detail. It is a confirmation of the deep ties between the climate movement and indigenous rights that has played a huge role in stopping pipelines in and from Canada. It has inspired and informed young people who may have half a century or more of good work yet to do. It has been a beacon whose meaning stretches beyond that time and place.

To know history is to be able to see beyond the present; to remember the past gives you capacity to look forward as well, to see that everything changes and the most dramatic changes are often the most unforeseen.

The 1970s antinuclear movement was a potent force in its time, now seldom remembered, though its influence is still with us. In her important book *Direct Action: Protest and the Reinvention of American Radicalism*, L. A. Kauffman reports that the first significant action against nuclear power, in 1976, was inspired by an extraordinary protest the previous year in West Germany, which had forced the government to abandon plans to build a nuclear reactor. A group that called itself the Clamshell Alliance arose to oppose building a nuclear power plant in New England. Despite creative tactics, great movement building, and extensive media coverage against the Seabrook nuclear power station in New Hampshire, the activists did not stop the plant. But they did inspire a sister organization, the Abalone Alliance in central California, which used similar strategies to try to stop the Diablo Canyon nuclear power plant.

The groups protested against two particular nuclear power plants; those two plants opened anyway. You can call that a failure, but Kauffman notes that the actions inspired people around the country to organize their own antinuclear groups, a movement that brought about the cancellation of more than one hundred planned nuclear projects over several years, raised public awareness, and changed public opinion about nuclear power. Then she gets into the really exciting part, writing that the Clamshell Alliance's "most striking legacy was in consolidating and promoting what became the dominant model for large-scale direct-action organizing for the next forty years.... It was picked up by ... the Pledge of Resistance, a nationwide network of groups organizing against US policy in Central America" in the 1980s.

"Hundreds more employed it that fall in a civil disobedience action to protest the supreme court's anti-gay *Bowers vs. Hardwick* sodomy decision," Kauffman continues. "The AIDS activist group ACT UP used a version of this model when it organized bold takeovers of the headquarters of the Food and Drug Administration in 1988 and the National Institutes of Health in 1990, to pressure both institutions to take swifter action toward approving experimental AIDS medication." And on, into the current millennium.

But what were the strategies and organizing principles the Clamshell organizers catalyzed? The short answer is nonviolent direct action externally, and consensus decision-making process internally. The former has a history that reaches around the world; the latter, one that stretches back to the early history of European dissidents in North America. That is, nonviolence is a strategy articulated by Gandhi, first used by residents of Indian descent to protest against discrimination in South Africa on September 11, 1906. The young lawyer's sense of possibility and power was expanded immediately afterward when he traveled to London to pursue his cause. Three days after he arrived, British women battling for the right to vote occupied the British Parliament, and eleven were arrested, refused to pay their fines, and were sent to prison. They made a deep impression on Gandhi.

He wrote about them in a piece titled "Deeds Better than Words," quoting Jane Cobden, the sister of one of the arrestees, who said, "I shall never obey any law in the making of which I have no hand; I will not accept the authority of the court executing those laws." Gandhi declared: "Today the whole country is laughing at them, and they have only a few people on their side. But undaunted, these women work on steadfast in their cause. They are bound to succeed and gain the franchise." And he saw that if they could win, so could the Indian citizens in British Africa fighting for their rights. In the same article (in 1906!) he prophesied: "When ... [the] time comes, India's bonds will snap of themselves."

Ideas are contagious, emotions are contagious, hope is contagious, courage is contagious. When we embody those qualities, or their opposites, we convey them to others.

That is to say, British suffragists, who won limited access to the vote for women in 1918 and full access in 1928, played a part in inspiring an Indian man who, twenty years later, led the liberation of the Asian subcontinent from British rule. He, in turn, inspired a Black man in the American South to study his ideas and their application. After a 1959 pilgrimage to India to meet with Gandhi's heirs, Martin Luther King wrote: "While the Montgomery boycott was going on, India's Gandhi was the guiding light of our technique of nonviolent social change. We spoke of him often." Those techniques, further developed by the civil rights movement, were taken up around the world, including in the struggle against apartheid, at one end of the African continent, and in the Arab Spring, at the other.

Participation in the civil rights movement of the early 1960s shaped many lives. One of them is John Lewis, one of the first Freedom Riders, a young leader of the lunch counter sit-ins, a victim of a brutal beating that broke his skull on the Selma march. Decades later, as a congressman, Lewis was one of the boldest in questioning Trump's legitimacy, and he led dozens of other Democratic members of Congress in boycotting the inauguration. When the attack on Muslim refugees and immigrants began a week after Trump's inauguration, Lewis showed up at the Atlanta airport to protest.

When those women were arrested in parliament, they were fighting for the right of British women to vote. They succeeded in liberating themselves. But they also passed along tactics, spirit, and defiance. You can trace a lineage backward to the antislavery movement that inspired the American women's suffrage movement, forward right up to John Lewis, standing up for refugees and Muslims in the Atlanta airport. We are carried along by the heroines and heroes who came before and opened the doors of possibility and imagination.

Michel Foucault noted, "People know what they do; frequently they know why they do what they do; but what they don't know is what what they do does." You do what you can. What you've done may do more than you can imagine for generations to come. You plant a seed and a tree grows from it; will there be fruit, shade, habitat for birds, more seeds, a forest, wood to build a cradle or a house? You don't know. A tree can live much longer than you. So will an idea, and sometimes the changes that result from accepting that new idea about what is true, or right, just might remake the world. You do what you can do; you do your best; what what you do does is not up to you.

That's a way to remember the legacy of the external practice of nonviolent civil disobedience used by the antinuclear movement of the 1970s, as with the civil rights movement of the 1960s, which did so much to expand and refine these techniques.

As for the internal process: in *Direct Action*, Kauffman addresses the Clamshell Alliance's influences, quoting a participant named Ynestra King: "Certain forms that had been learned from feminism were just naturally introduced into the situation and a certain ethos of respect, which was reinforced by the Quaker tradition." Sukie Rice and Elizabeth Boardman, early participants in the Clamshell Alliance, as Kauffman relates, were influenced by the Quakers, and they brought the Quaker practice of consensus decision-making to the new group: "The idea was to ensure that no one's voice was silenced, that there was no division between leaders and followers." The Quakers have, since the seventeenth century, been radical dissidents who opposed war, hierarchical structures, and much else. An organizer named Joanne Sheehan said, "While nonviolence training, doing actions in small groups, and agreeing to a set of nonviolence guidelines were not new, it was new to blend them in combination with a commitment to consensus decision-making and a non-hierarchical structure." They were making a way of operating and organizing that spread throughout the progressive activist world.

There are terrible stories about how viruses like HIV jump species and mutate. There are also ideas and tactics that jump communities and mutate, to our benefit. There is an evil term, *collateral damage*, for the noncombatants killed in war as a sort of byproduct of war's violence. Maybe what I am proposing here is an idea of collateral benefit.

What we call democracy is often a majority rule that leaves the minority, even 49.9 percent of the people—or more, if it's a three-way vote—out in the cold. Consensus leaves no one out. After Clamshell, it jumped into radical politics and reshaped them, making them more generously inclusive and egalitarian. And it's been honed and refined and used by nearly every movement I've been a part of or witnessed—from the antinuclear actions at the Nevada test site in the 1980s and 1990s to the organization of the shutdown of the World Trade Organization meetings in Seattle in late 1999, a victory against neoliberalism that changed the fate of the world, to Occupy Wall Street in 2011 and after.

So what did the Clamshell Alliance achieve? Everything but its putative goal. It provided tools to change the world, over and over, and a vision of a more egalitarian, inclusive way to use those tools. There are crimes against humanity, crimes against nature, and other forms of destruction that we need to stop as rapidly as possible, and the endeavors to do so are under way. They are informed by these earlier activists, equipped with the tools they developed. But the efforts against these things can have a longer legacy, if we learn to recognize collateral benefits and indirect effects.

If you are a member of civil society, if you demonstrate and call your representatives and donate to human rights campaigns, you will see politicians and judges and the powerful take or be given credit for the changes you effected, sometimes after they'd initially resisted and opposed them. You will have to believe in your own power and impact anyway. You will have to keep in mind that many of our greatest victories are what doesn't happen: what isn't built or destroyed, deregulated or legitimized, passed into law or tolerated in the culture. Things disappear because of our efforts and we forget they were there, which is a way to forget that we tried and won.

Even losing can be part of the process: as the bills to abolish slavery in the British Empire failed over and over again, the ideas behind them spread until, twenty-seven years after the first bill was introduced, a version finally passed. We have to remember that the media usually likes to tell simple, direct stories in which, if a court rules or an elective body passes a law, that action reflects the actors' own beneficence or insight or evolution. They will seldom go further to explore how that perspective was shaped by the nameless and unsung, by the people whose actions built up a new world or worldview the way that innumerable corals build a reef.

The only power adequate to stop tyranny and destruction is civil society, which is the great majority of us when we remember our power and come together. The job begins with opposition to specific instances of destruction, but it is not ended until we have made deep systemic changes and recommitted ourselves, not just as a revolution, because revolutions don't last, but as a civil society with values of equality, democracy, inclusion, full participation—a radical *e pluribus unum*, plus compassion. This work is always, first and last, storytelling work, or what some of my friends call "the battle of the story." Building, remembering, retelling, celebrating our own stories is part of our work.

This work will only matter if it's sustained. To sustain it, people have to believe that the myriad small, incremental actions matter. That they matter even when the consequences aren't immediate or obvious. They must remember that often when you fail at your immediate objective—to block a nominee or a pipeline or to pass a bill—that, even then, you may have changed the whole framework in ways that make broader change more possible. You may change the story or the rules, give tools, templates, or encouragement to future activists, and make it possible for those around you to persist in their efforts.

To believe it matters—well, we can't see the future, but we have the past. Which gives us patterns, models, parallels, principles, and resources; stories of heroism, brilliance, and persistence; and the deep joy to be found in doing the work that matters. With those in hand, we can seize the possibilities and begin to make hopes into actualities.

Acknowledgments

Writing is done in solitude but it is by no means made in isolation. In that solitude I find the quiet to think and respond to the world and the things people have said, and everything I write is in conversation with others. The essays in this book evolved out of adventures and ongoing conversations with the people most important to me. My thanks go out to: Taj James, Erica Chenoweth, Jon Wiener, Astra Taylor, Sam Green, Marina Sitrin, Antonia Juhasz, L. A. Kauffman, Joan Halifax, Gavin Browning, Joshua Jelly-Schapiro, Garnette Cadogan, Cleve Jones, Maurice Ruffin, Alan Senauke, Melody Chavis, and many others with whom I've ruminated, marched, hoped, and worried over the past few years. A special thanks goes to the climate activists I've been blessed to work alongside these past several years, including May Boeve, Anna Goldstein, David Solnit and Bill McKibben of 350.org.; Steve Kretzmann and the crew at Oil Change International, on whose board I now serve, with pride, and my old friend and new fellow board member Renato Redentor Constantino. And my apologies to so many people I have overlooked.

Of course once something's written, it goes to an editor to be published, and I've been lucky to have as editors for these essays Dorothy Wickenden at the *New Yorker*, John Freeman and Jonny

Diamond at Lithub, the excellent gang at the *London Review of Books*, Christopher Beha (to whom an extra dose of gratitude is due for hiring me to write the Easy Chair column in 2014) and Emily Cooke at *Harper's*, Amana Fontanella-Khan and Merope Mills at the *Guardian*, and at Haymarket Books, Anthony Arnove and Caroline Luft.

Special thanks for talking to me about Alejandro Nieto go to Elvira and Refugio Nieto, Adriana Camarena, Ely Flores, Oscar Salinas, Ben Bac Sierra, and Jorge Del Rio, and to Sana Saleem, who worked alongside me to report the story of the trial and the murder. And more thanks for an early education in thinking outside the Judeo-Christian box to Lewis DeSoto, long ago.

The essay "Break the Story" was given as a commencement address at my alma mater, the Graduate School of Journalism at UC Berkeley, and I'm grateful both for the honor of talking to an extraordinary group of graduating journalists and for the superb education I received there long ago, in ethics as well as in reporting and law and resourcefulness.

As for Jarvis Masters, who continues to be a cherished friend and a stunning model of grace under extraordinary grimness, I regret that my writing on him in this book doesn't convey how funny he is and how much fun we have talking. He has produced many kinds of liberation during his imprisonment, and that is a beautiful thing.

And, as ever, thanks to C.

About Haymarket Books

Haymarket Books is a nonprofit, progressive book distributor and publisher, a project of the Center for Economic Research and Social Change. We believe that activists need to take ideas, history, and politics into the many struggles for social justice today. Learning the lessons of past victories, as well as defeats, can arm a new generation of fighters for a better world. As Karl Marx said, "The philosophers have merely interpreted the world; the point, however, is to change it."

We could not succeed in our publishing efforts without the generous financial support of our readers. Learn more and shop our full catalog online at www.haymarketbooks.org.

Also Available by Rebecca Solnit

Hope in the Dark: Untold Histories, Wild Possibilities

Men Explain Things to Me

The Mother of All Questions

Also Available
from Haymarket Books

The Battle for Paradise: Puerto Rico Takes on the Disaster Capitalists
Naomi Klein

Capitalism: A Ghost Story
Arundhati Roy

The End of Imagination
Arundhati Roy

Exoneree Diaries: The Fight for Innocence, Independence, and Identity
Alison Flowers

Freedom Is a Constant Struggle: Ferguson, Palestine,
and the Foundations of a Movement
Angela Y. Davis, edited by Frank Barat,
foreword by Dr. Cornel West

How We Get Free: Black Feminism and the Combahee River Collective
Edited by Keeanga-Yamahtta Taylor

Night Thoughts
Wallace Shawn

On Palestine
Noam Chomsky and Ilan Pappé, edited by Frank Barat

The Speech: The Story Behind Dr. Martin Luther King Jr.'s Dream
Gary Younge

Things That Make White People Uncomfortable
Michael Bennett and Dave Zirin, foreword by Martellus Bennett

About the Author

© ADRIAN MENDOZA

Writer, historian, and activist Rebecca Solnit is the author of twenty or so books on feminism, Western and indigenous history, popular power, social change and insurrection, wandering and walking, hope and disaster, including *Men Explain Things to Me* and *Hope in the Dark*, both also with Haymarket; a trilogy of atlases of American cities; *The Faraway Nearby*; *A Paradise Built in Hell: The Extraordinary Communities That Arise in Disaster*; *A Field Guide to Getting Lost*; *Wanderlust: A History of Walking*; and *River of Shadows: Eadweard Muybridge and the Technological Wild West* (for which she received a Guggenheim, the National Book Critics Circle Award in criticism, and the Lannan Literary Award). A product of the California public education system from kindergarten to graduate school, she is a regular contributor to the *Guardian*.